Dan Colwell

JPMGUIDES

Contents

This Way Milan

Italy's Powerhouse

Capital of Lombardy, the richest region in Italy, and famously proficient at the business of making money, Milan has long considered itself to be different from the rest of the country. Here, they say, everything functions properly and the people are hard-working. A lunch hour might last only an hour and a half instead of an entire afternoon, the transport system runs smoothly and the city gleams. Milan is a magnet for all manner of business; it's home to automobile, aircraft, electronics and fashion industries. It is the centre of Italian banking and commerce, and also dominates Italy's new high-tech media, computer and telecommunications industries. Here is a city that more than pays its way: with less than 5 per cent of the population, Milan generates a staggering 25 per cent of the country's tax revenues. While Rome rests on its history and Venice is sinking into its canals, this vibrant, independent and modern-minded metropolis, as the Milanese see it, has spearheaded the revival of the Italian nation, looks out to the world, and confidently faces up to the economic and political challenges of the new millennium.

Perhaps it's a relief to find that this portrait of an un-Italian, hard-nosed business city isn't the whole picture. The fact is, the Milanese know how to enjoy *la dolce vita* every bit as much as the Romans and the Neapolitans. Less demonstrative about it, they have busily engaged themselves in organizing their society the better to achieve it.

As a result, Milan offers its visitors the best of two worlds. An almost Germanic pride in getting things done efficiently has been happily united with the quintessential Latin passion for food, fashion and football, at which the city excels. Milan's difference from Italy, one might say, makes it a triumphant success at the very business of being Italian.

City of Culture

While renowned for its financial clout, Milan generally suffers by comparison with Rome, Venice and Tuscany when it comes to cultural treasures. But there are plenty of surprises in store for those who come here expecting it to be all stylish clothing and little artistic substance. First and foremost, Milan is home to Leonardo da Vinci's *Last Supper*, one of the world's most famous and 3 evocative paintings. Recently restored, it adorns the refectory wall of Santa Maria delle Grazie, an exquisite Renaissance church. The 15th-century Castello Sforzesco houses an art museum, with a superb collection of major Italian paintings and, as its centrepiece, Michelangelo's extraordinary *Pietà Rondanini*, a nine-year work-in-progress that he was still sculpting a few days before his death. In the city centre, the Biblioteca Ambrosiana displays a rare Leonardo portrait, Raphael's cartoons of the School of Athens and one of Caravaggio's sardonic still-life paintings, where the bowl of fruit is already worm-ravaged. But most impressive of all is the great Brera gallery, one of Italy's premier museums. Established by Napoleon during his brief reign as the King of Italy (he had with typical modesty crowned himself in the Duomo), it is crammed with art he'd looted from Lombardy's churches and *palazzi*, and can boast everything from Renaissance masters to 20th-century experimentalists. Milan can proudly take its place among the world's top cultural cities.

Alluring Lakes

One of the great features of Milan is the accessibility of Italy's spectacular Lake District. Nestling in the foothills of the Alps, a short distance north of the city, the lakes were formed during the last Ice Age by huge glaciers sliding down from the mountains and gouging out deep valleys, the basins of which later filled with melted ice.

Their proximity to the snow-capped Alps not only gives them a majestic—and highly photogenic—backdrop, but also a remarkable microclimate. The mountains act as a vast insulating barrier, preventing cold north European weather from reaching them. Thus winters can be mild, and the almost Mediterranean atmosphere is enhanced by glamorous resorts, with grand hotels, fine restaurants, palm-shaded waterfront promenades and a profusion of oleander, rhododendron, olive and lemon trees.

Such wonders of nature have inevitably been a major attraction for poets and artists, from 1st-century Romans, such as Pliny the Younger and Catullus, to the Romantics Stendhal and Shelley and 20th-century D.H. Lawrence and Henry James (who thought the beauty of the lakes beyond description). Nowadays, more than just a few artists have discovered the delights of the Lake District. Undoubtedly crowded, they still retain their ability to overawe the most world-weary onlooker and, for a moment, make poets of us all.

Around 600 BC, the Insubres, a Celtic tribe from Gaul, made their way to the lush river valley of the Po and founded a capital city on the site of Milan. They were ousted in 222 BC, when the Romans conquered the region. Mediolanum, as the city was then known, rapidly developed into the most important trading town in Cisalpine Gaul (the Romans' name for their lands on the south side of the Alps). Under Emperor Augustus, it acquired the status of the Empire's second city, while the nearby lakes became a favourite holiday destination for the Roman upper crust.

The increasing disintegration of the Empire at the end of the 3rd century AD only enhanced the city's prestige. Due to its strategic position on Italy's frontier with the rest of Europe, Mediolanum was chosen by Diocletian as the Empire's new administrative and military centre. His successor, Constantine, used the Edict of Milan in 313 to proclaim freedom of worship for Christians and to pave the way for Christianity to become the dominant European religion. Later in the century, Milan's reputation as an important Christian city was assured through the eloquence and pres-

tige of Bishop Ambrose, who famously refused to be intimidated by the Emperor Theodosius. With the final collapse of the Roman Empire in the 5th century, however, Milan faced a dramatic reversal of fortune.

Huns, Goths and Lombards

No longer protected by Roman power, Milan was open to attack by barbarian tribes from across the Alps. The most infamous barbarian of them all, Attila the Hun, devastated the city in 452. But there was little to choose between him and his rivals. Just as Milan was recovering from his visit, the Goths turned up in 539 and destroyed it again. Exhausted by such a battering, the Milanese were unable to put up much of a fight when only 30 years later the Langobardi—better known as the Lombards—invaded.

The Lombards came from Germany, and the name has been variously ascribed to their habit of wearing long beards or their penchant for carrying long *bardi*—a type of axe. Unlike their predecessors, their intention wasn't simply to plunder and move on, but rather to set up a Lombard kingdom. With Milan in ruins, they established their capital in

Pavia. Brutal and bloody rulers, they founded nonetheless a law school in Pavia and set up a system of law courts. Their grip on power lasted until 774, when the last Lombard king was deposed by his son-in-law Charlemagne, who incorporated Lombardy into the Frankish dominions.

The Middle Ages

During the 9th and 10th centuries, the irrepressible Milanese began to revive. In 1045, partly in reaction to the increasing power and authoritarian character of the Bishops of Milan, the citizens took political matters into their own hands by declaring their city a *comune*, a commune with an autonomous government.

Over the next 100 years, the newly assertive Milanese ran roughshod over rival Lombard cities, razing Lodi and Como and defeating Pavia and Cremona in battle. But Northern Italy's combination of wealth and warring disunity soon attracted the attention of bigger fish. Under the pretext of acting as a peacemaker between Milan and its neighbours, the German Emperor Frederick Barbarossa crossed the Alps seeking to coerce Milan into

Since Roman times, the lush Lake District has inspired artists, poets and gardeners.

his Holy Roman Empire. The Milanese went back to war as soon as he left, so to show them who was boss he returned in 1162 and levelled the city.

It proved to be a Pyrrhic victory for Barbarossa, for its main achievement was to demonstrate to the Lombard cities that they were in danger of losing their independence to him. Remarkably, the Milanese rebuilt their city and were able to assume leadership of the Lombard League within four years. At the Battle of Legnano in 1176, the League decisively defeated Barbarossa's German troops, and at the subsequent Peace of Constance in 1183, Milan regained all its former privileges as a *comune*. The result was a century of relentless economic success, with the development of powerful new guilds of wool and armaments workers.

Viscontis and Sforzas

The 13th century saw the growth of difficult internal pressures. A dangerous division formed between the Guelfs, who supported the pope and were drawn mainly from the guild workers, and the Ghibellines, who thought it politic to follow the new Holy Roman Emperor, Frederick II. The two factions rallied around different families, the Torrianis and the Viscontis. The Torrianiled Guelfs were eventually defeated by the Ghibelline forces under Archbishop Ottone Visconti at Desio in 1277. By 1311, his nephew Matteo Visconti had replaced the privileges of the *comune* with the autocratic and dynastical rule of the *signoria*, or lordship.

Backed up by the Holy Roman Empire, and helped by a rapid development of the economy, the Viscontis were able to maintain a ruthless grip on the city. They reached their highwater mark under Gian Galeazzo Visconti, who ruled from 1385 to 1402. A powerful politician and soldier, he conquered vast tracts of Northern Italy but was also a patron of the arts and a modernizer of government. Not without social pretensions either, he bought the title of Duke of Milan from the emperor in 1395. The danger of so much power being invested in one figure became apparent when Gian Galeazzo died of plague in 1402. His weak and unstable successor, Giovanni Maria, proved unequal to the task of controlling Milan's competing political forces, and by 1447 the Visconti line had died out.

A three-year experiment in republicanism was brought to a close with the advent of Francesco Sforza, an ambitious mercenary soldier, or *condottiere*. Sforza's dubious claim to the title of Duke of Milan lay in his marriage to an illegitimate daughter of the Visconti family. But he and his son, Ludovico il Moro, were more than able to live up to the Visconti style of rule, for like all true Renaissance princes they were a Machiavellian mixture of tyrant at home, wily diplomat abroad, and cultural benefactor at all times, no matter what the expense. At this time, Milan was embarked on another period of prosperity based on the silk industry. With the taxes extracted by the Sforza court, Milan flowered as a Renaissance city, with Donato Bramante and Leonardo da Vinci executing some of their best work there.

Ludovico's reign was to end in disaster. One of his many diplo-

1

THE BEST ROMAN RUIN The **Grotte di Catullo**, on the tip of Lake Garda's Sirmione peninsula, was the 1st-century BC holiday home of a mega-rich Roman. There's a profusion of mosaics, columns and capitals, plus spectacular views of the lake.

matic schemes was to encourage the French king, Charles VIII, to invade Naples, Milan's enemy. The ease with which Charles succeeded revealed the vulnerability of the various Italian states. Desperate rearguard action to get rid of the French proved too little, too late. Over the next 40 years, Milan became the victim of a political tug-of-war, with Ludovico losing the duchy to Charles's successor Louis XII, then going back and forth between the French and the Sforzas. Things came to a head in 1535 when the avaricious Charles V, king of Spain and Holy Roman Emperor since 1519, pressed his claim on Milan and brought it under Habsburg rule.

Life under the Habsburgs

The Habsburgs replaced the dynamism and turmoil of the Renaissance era with political stability but a stifling conservatism. After only five years, Charles handed the city over to his son, the future Philip II of Spain, patron of the Counter-Reformation and its agents, the Inquisition. Although this was dedicated to crushing free intellectual enquiry, Milan benefited once more from having an enlightened Bishop, Charles Borromeo (1538–84), who promoted educational and welfare institutions and was canonized in 1610. The effects of Habsburg rule, coupled with devastating plagues in 1576 and 1630, caused Milan to enter a period of political and economic stagnation that lasted till the end of Spanish rule in 1706.

Following the decline of Spanish power, the Austrian Habsburgs took control of Milan under Prince Eugene of Savoy. The city fared better under the Austrian branch of the family, and as the 18th century wore on, the economy revived. Milan's distinctive neoclassical monuments—most notably the great opera house, La Scala—were built during this period. However, the Milanese still felt oppressed, and when the republican French Army under Napoleon routed the Austrians in 1796, they were welcomed as liberators.

Napoleon in Milan

Napoleon's influence on the city was typically dramatic. In 1797, he set up a Cisalpine Republic, with its own constitution and Milan as its capital. Eight years later, he crowned himself King of Italy in the Duomo, and Milan became the capital of the new kingdom. The city underwent a full Napoleonic makeover. Extensive public works were carried out, the legal and education systems reformed and church property expropriated. This was facilitated by a considerable amount

Far from the city bustle, Santa Maria delle Grazie is a delightful Renaissance setting for Leonardo da Vinci's Last Supper.

of arm-twisting, high taxes and pure theft, but it's fair to say that Milan never recovered from Napoleon's time at the helm. When the Austrians re-entered the city following the collapse of his empire in 1814, they found their hosts filled with a desire for self-determination.

Risorgimento

Milan took a prominent role in the *risorgimento*, the mid-century nationalist movement for Italian unity. In 1848, the city rose against the Austrians in what became known as the Cinque Giornate (five day) rebellion. Milan's liberation lasted for several months before the Austrians were able to regain control of the city, but opposition to Habsburg rule continued. The Austrians were finally defeated at the Battle of Magenta in 1859. Vittorio Emanuele II of Savoy entered Milan in triumph with his ally Napoleon III. In 1861 he was officially proclaimed king of a united, independent Italy.

The stage was set for an Italian industrial revolution, which, with its powerful new metal and chemical industries, Milan was quickly able to lead. The city assumed a dominant position in the nation's economy that it has never relinquished since.

The 20th Century

Although from 1870 Rome was the political centre of the new nation, Milan's dynamic character meant that it was the crucible of radical politics. The first Italian socialist party began there in 1882, and during the 1890s, left and right vied for power. An economic depression led to food riots, and at one demonstration in 1896, more than 100 people were killed. Prosperity was restored in the blissful years of calm prior to World War I, but out of that cataclysm sprang dangerous nationalist forces. In March 1919, Mussolini founded the Fasci di Combattimento, the Fascist movement, which intimidated left-wing parties around Milan.

Mussolini became dictator of Italy in 1922. His promise of order and willingness to spend on weapons and machinery suited Milan's big businesses. During World War II, the presence of that same heavy industry made Milan the target for Allied bombing raids in 1943. Mussolini fell from power later in the year and was sent to the north, establishing a German-backed puppet government at Salò on Lake Garda. He was shot in April 1945 by the Italian partisans, and his body was strung up along with that of his mistress, Clara Petacci, from the roof of a petrol station on the Piazza Loreto.

The post-war period has witnessed a characteristic Milanese recovery, with a business and industry-driven economic miracle propelling Italy's revival. As such, the region has attracted large numbers of Italians from the poorer south looking for work. The increasing importance of the European Union has only added to the region's wealth, as Milan is perfectly situated to profit from a free-trade area dominated by its near-neighbours in Germany and France.

In recent years, however, the shine has been taken off the Milanese success story by a remarkable bribery scandal that broke in 1993, earning Milan the name Tangentopoli—Bribe City. This touched the two main political parties, the Socialists and the Christian Democrats, as well as business leaders. One of the results has been a move away from mainstream politics in Milan. The right-wing Lombard League, campaigning on a platform of greater autonomy for Lombardy, won the mayoral elections in Milan in 1993. A year later it joined a coalition government with Silvio Berlusconi (a Milanese media mogul), and his Forza Italia party.

Despite the scandal and the intrigue, Milan continues in its favourite role as the capital in all but name of modern Italy.

On the Scene

Milan's superb galleries, ancient churches, first-rate restaurants and smart shopping streets are concentrated in a surprisingly small area around the centre. Only a short distance away from the city are the sparkling resorts and glorious scenery of Italy's Lake District, easily reached from Milan via a fast network of motorways. The lakes are encircled by small, winding roads with what seems an endless series of breathtaking vistas.

▶ MILAN

Piazza del Duomo, West of the Duomo, Castello Sforzesco, From La Scala to the Brera, North of the Centre, South of the Centre

At the ancient core of this vast, fast-paced modern city lie the major sights—the Duomo, the church of Santa Maria delle Grazie housing da Vinci's *Last Supper*, the Castello and the Brera. Around each of these stars are some fascinating satellites that more than repay a visit, such as the Pinacoteca Ambrosiana, or the entertaining Science Museum, with its models based on da Vinci's inventions. Most of these sights are within walking distance

Soaring heavenwards, the gilded Madonna on the Duomo is affectionately called La Madunina.

of the Duomo, but if the streets become too exhausting, you can always hop onto the metro.

Piazza del Duomo

The cathedral square is Milan's spiritual centre. Constantly crisscrossed by the city's hurrying workers, it's a meeting place and hang-out for the Milanese young and a magnet for tourists. The piazza is ringed with some fine 19th-century arcades, not least the remarkable neo-Renaissance Galleria. A bronze equestrian statue of King Vittorio Emanuele II stands in front of the cathedral. Here, too, jostle the pigeon-feed sellers and ice-cream vendors, 13 and there are several cafés ideal for people-watching. With undoubtedly one of the most dramatic cityscapes in Italy, the Piazza del Duomo is a place you will return to again and again.

Duomo

This is a marvel of Gothic fantasy, expressed in marble turrets, 135 carved pinnacles and extravagant flying buttresses. The tallest spire carries a gilded 18th-century statue of the Madonna that's illuminated at night, while 2,245 statues adorn the roof and façade, with another 2,000 inside. Now and at least until 2006, the façade is undergoing restoration and swathed in scaffolding.

The cathedral was begun in 1386 as a votive offering by Duke Gian Galeazzo Visconti, who hoped he would be rewarded with a son. His prayers were answered, but the boy was the ineffectual Giovanni Maria, whose failings hastened the fall of the Viscontis.

The cathedral itself would take more than 500 years to complete. The ambitious scope of the building flummoxed local architects, and master-builders from all around Europe had to be drafted in to help execute the plans. The great triangular façade was completed only in 1813 under Napoleon's orders, and other exterior sculptures were still being added in the 20th century.

Inside the Duomo, 52 immense columns mark out a nave of five aisles and soar upwards from the dazzling, patterned floor, creating a stunning sense of space. It is lit by daylight filtering through magnificent stained-glass windows, the oldest of which date from the 15th century and are on the right-hand side. Just inside the main entrance, you can go down to the excavated 4th-century baptistery of an earlier church, where in 387 Bishop Ambrose baptised St Augustine.

Further along, in the right transept, look out for a famously

THE TWO BEST FESTIVALS You can sample the parties and parades of Milan's **Mardi Gras Carnival** just before the start of Lent. On Lake Como's Isola Comacina each June, there's the spectacular **Feast of San Giovanni**, with fireworks, boat procession, locals in 18th-century costume and illuminations made from thousands of snail shells turned into tiny lamps.

gruesome statue of St Bartholomew, sculpted by Marco d'Agrate in 1562. It shows the saint, who has just been flayed alive, carrying his skin over his shoulder. Here, too, is Leone Leoni's fine Renaissance monument to Gian Giacomo de' Medici. A nearby entrance beneath the main altar leads down to the crypt, where an octagonal baroque vault houses the remains of St Charles Borromeo, the great 16th-century counter-Reformation Bishop of Milan.

The best way to round off a visit to the Duomo is to ascend to the rooftop, but unfortunately it is closed during the ongoing restoration. You'll have to come back in a few years' time to see the amazing close-up view of this wonderland forest of spires, and the far-reaching panorama.

Galleria Vittorio Emanuele

The industrial age's riposte to the Duomo is this spectacular cruciform shopping arcade, built mainly of iron and glass in neo-Renaissance style. It was designed by Giuseppe Mengoni, who, a few days before it opened in 1878, fell from the roof to his death. The building's grand, high arched entrance opens off the colonnaded north side of the Piazza del Duomo. Inside are fashionable boutiques, bookshops and some of the city's most elegant cafés, such as Zucca's and Savini, which provide unbeatable spots for sipping an aperitif and watching all Milan stroll by.

Piazza Mercanti

Situated just off the northwest edge of the cathedral square, this small piazza is one of the last remnants of medieval Milan. As the city's central market, it once buzzed with the activities of deal-making merchants. Now, rather more sedate booksellers occupy the Romanesque Palazzo della Ragione (1233), the ancient civic hall and magistrate's court. A fine 13th-century equestrian sculpture adorns the south wall, while the extra storey on top was added courtesy of the Austrians in 1771. Across from here, the Gothic Loggia degli Osii dates from 1316 and was built out of black and white marble.

Palazzo Reale

On the south side of the cathedral, the former Royal Palace was the seat of Visconti rule in the 14th century, and later used by Milan's Spanish and Austrian governors, who had the neoclassical façade constructed in the 1770s.

Part of the ground floor now houses the Museo del Duomo, with a superb display of art, sculpture, tapestries and stained glass taken from the cathedral over the past six centuries. 15

In the main part of the palace, the Civico Museo d'Arte Contemporanea (CIMAC) has a noteworthy collection of modern Italian art, including works by Boccioni, de Chirico, Modigliani, Morandi and Carlo Carrà.

Ospedale Maggiore

From behind the Palazzo Reale, continue south past the ornate 14th-century belltower of the San Gottardo church, to this huge Renaissance hospital, now part of the Università degli Studi di Milano (Via Festa del Perdono). It was the brainchild of Francesco Sforza, who commissioned the Florentine architect Antonio Filarete to design a building to house all of Milan's hospitals under one roof. Begun in 1456, the distinctive terracotta brick frontage was subsequently altered and added to. The best place for seeing Filarete's work as he intended it is in the Ospedale's series of impressive cloisters. The nearby cafés and bars are popular with students and always very lively.

San Satiro

The unobtrusive 19th-century entrance on Via Torino, reached from the southwest corner of the Piazza del Duomo, conceals a jewel of Renaissance church architecture. This is the first Milanese work by the great Donato Bramante, begun in 1478 on the site of a much earlier church. The cramped interior feels quite spacious, an effect created by Bramante's masterstroke—a *trompe l'œil* of stucco pilasters behind the altar making the apse seem much deeper than it really is. The Cappella della Pietà, in the left transept, incorporates part of the original 9th-century church, while Bramante's delightful octagonal baptistery is entered from the right-hand aisle. The best exterior view of the Cappella, as well as the church's classic 11th-century Lombardian *campanile*, is from Via Falcone.

West of the Duomo

Beyond Milan's business district lies the Santa Maria delle Grazie church, a shrine for art lovers the world over. But there are many other fascinating sights in this area, not least the Romanesque church of Sant'Ambrogio and the Museum of Science and Technology, with its intriguing models of Leonardo's inventions.

Pinacoteca Ambrosiana

A short distance north of San Satiro, on Piazza Pio XI, the Ambrosiana is a vast library and art gallery. It was established in 1618 by Federico Borromeo, cousin of the famous Bishop of Milan, and located in the family's magnificent *palazzo*. The library contains 750,000 books and 35,000 precious manuscripts, including a mid 14th-century edition of the *Divine Comedy*, and Leonardo's sketchbooks know as the *Codex Atlanticus*.

The art gallery, or Pinacoteca, is one of Milan's best. Here you'll find Leonardo's quintessential Renaissance *Portrait of a Musician*, together with works by his Milanese followers, such as Bernardino Luini and Ambrogio de Predis. Not to be missed is Caravaggio's post-Edenic depiction of a basket of worm-eaten fruit, thought to be the first Italian still-life; Raphael's preparatory cartoon for the School of Athens fresco in the Vatican; and canvasses by Tintoretto, Botticelli, Titian and Bramantino.

Museo Archeologico

On Corso Magenta, this collection of Etruscan, Greek and Roman archaeological discoveries is housed in the attractive 16th-century Monastero Maggiore. The adjoining San Maurizio church has a chapel decorated with Bernardino Luini's powerful fresco of the *Martyrdom of St Catherine*.

Santa Maria delle Grazie

Thousands of people come here to see Leonardo's *Ultima Cena*—the Last Supper—but the church (Via Caradosso, just off Corso Magenta) is a superb Renaissance work of art in itself. The mid-15th century Gothic frame was revamped by Donato Bramante, who added the sumptuous terracotta and stone decoration in 1492.

There's a separate entrance into the refectory, where Leonardo's great mural has miraculously survived not only the mishandling of Napoleon's troops, who used the building to stable their

---

HAIR TODAY, GONE TOMORROW

Some of the Ambrosiana's more unusual exhibits might not qualify as high art, but they're undoubtedly just as intriguing as the more exalted works on display. Top of the list are the gloves Napoleon wore at the Battle of Waterloo and a lock of Lucrezia Borgia's gold-coloured hair. This was kept unsupervised in the library downstairs until the day Lord Byron showed up in town. The poet visited the Ambrosiana and read some letters written by Lucrezia (who'd been married for a spell during the 1490s to one of the Sforzas). Lost in the romance of the occasion, he stole a strand of the hair as a trophy, which is why the rest of the lock is now kept upstairs protected from the prying fingers of other incurable Romantics.

La Scala, one of the world's greatest opera houses, is now undergoing a complete overhaul, to a design by Swiss architect Mario Botta.

horses, but also World War II bombing. More damaging, however, was Leonardo's decision to experiment with oil-based paint rather than the established fresco technique. The damp of the walls meant it began to flake off almost immediately. Several restorations later, there's very little left of the artist's original colours. The recent overhaul has left the fresco looking almost as good as new. But some art critics are unhappy that the last traces of Leonardo's hand have been eradicated.

It's up to each viewer to judge for himself, but undoubtedly the *Last Supper* (1495–97) still packs a considerable emotional punch.

Capturing the moment when Christ announces that one of the disciples will betray him, the scene is a masterly study in psychology. A resolute Christ, already relinquishing earthly concerns, sits immobile at the centre of a group that is all movement and hand gesture; the faces of the disciples reflect a variety of responses, from grief and anger to affronted innocence and Judas's insidious bravado.

On the opposite wall of the refectory is the somewhat overshadowed *Crucifixion*, painted in 1495 by Donato Montorfano. The colours here have been far better preserved.

Museum of Science and Technology

Head south across Corso Magenta to the Via San Vittore, where the impressively named Leonardo da Vinci Museo Nazionale della Scienza e della Tecnologia is located in the ancient San Vittore convent. There are several interesting rooms dedicated to clocks, music, arms manufacture, trains and boats, but the centrepiece is the Leonardo da Vinci Gallery, where the great man's weird and wonderful schemes—such as a mechanical drum to lead troops into battle—have been realised in model form.

Sant'Ambrogio

At the eastern end of Via San Vittore, this historic basilica was consecrated by Bishop Ambrose in 386. The shorter of the two towers was erected in the 9th century, while the taller Lombard Romanesque tower and porticoed atrium date from the 12th century.

The interior has several fine features. On the left-hand side of the church, a handsome pulpit, sculpted in 1080, covers a 4th-century Romano-Christian sarcophagus. The canopy over the altar is mounted on porphyry pillars, while the altar itself is a masterpiece in gold and silver crafted in 835. The crypt, entered from the sides of the presbytery, has the remains of St Ambrose.

Located in a section of the portico, the museum contains some fine medieval church treasures, frescoes by Luini and Bergognone, and even St Ambrose's bed.

POLITICIAN AND SAINT

Almost as soon as Christianity became the main religion of the Roman Empire, it faced the Arian heresy, which denied that Jesus was equal to God. Ambrose (Ambrogio) was a Roman governor sent to Milan in 374 to supervise the election of a new bishop at the height of this theological turmoil. Following a speech he'd made trying to calm the crowds, a cry went up, "Ambrose is the Bishop". He wasn't even baptised at the time, but within eight days he'd become a Christian and was made Bishop of Milan.

Ambrose's considerable prestige and famous oratorical skills are credited with holding the Christian church together at this early stage in its history. Such is his popularity that the Milanese are still known as Ambrosiani, after their patron saint. You'll see his symbols in some of Milan's churches—a swarm of bees denoting his honey-tongued eloquence and a whip portraying his suppression of the Arian heresy.

Castello Sforzesco

Northwest of Piazza del Duomo, the indomitable, red-brick castle, built by the Viscontis and reconstructed by the Sforzas, looms over the city. Enter through the central tower, designed by Antonio Filarete in 1454, to the vast Piazza d'Armi, where the Sforza troops once trained. On the far side is the Corte Ducale, the superb Renaissance apartments of the Sforzas, with decorations by Leonardo. Today they house the various Musei del Castello (castle museums).

Ancient Art

The Arte Antica section has an engrossingly diverse collection: Roman sculptures and sarcophagi, 16th and 17th-century tapestries, and the magnificent equestrian tomb of Bernabò Visconti, carved by Bonino da Campione in the 14th century. The grand finale is Michelangelo's last sculpture, the *Pietà Rondanini,* a powerful work that the artist was still sculpting just before his death at the age of 89.

Pinacoteca

On the upper storey, beyond a collection of Renaissance furnishings, the Pinacoteca has a surprisingly extensive gallery of 15th–18th-century art. There are paintings of the *Madonna and Child* by Giovanni Bellini and his brother-in-law, Mantegna, works by Veronese, Titian, Filippo Lippi and Canaletto, and several Lombardian contributions, most notably from Bergognone, Vincenzo Foppa and Boltraffio. Be sure to search out Arcimboldo's famous *Primavera*, a portrait of a woman's head composed entirely of flowers and fruit.

Across from here, in the Rocchetta Courtyard, are collections of ancient Egyptian artefacts, prehistoric archaeological finds from the Lombardy region, and musical instruments.

Parco Sempione

Behind the castle, the large park was the private hunting ground of the Dukes of Milan. Landscaped for public use as a park in the 19th century, it provides a welcome green space in the heart of the city. At the far end, the Arco della Pace is Milan's own version of Paris's more famous triumphal arch, built during Napoleon's rule in 1807.

From La Scala to the Brera

On the north side of the Galleria Vittorio Emanuele lies one of the world's great musical venues, La Scala—currently hidden behind scaffolding and hoardings as it is undergoing much needed modernization. From here, an enjoyable walk through grand boulevards and past impressive neo-classical *palazzi* brings you to the mighty Brera gallery.

Teatro alla Scala

The opera house was built under the Habsburgs in 1778 on the site of an old church, Santa Maria della Scala, from which it took its name. Its current renovation, by the Swiss architect Mario Botta, is the subject of great controversy as the stage and backstage area have been completely demolished and redesigned. However, the façade, the foyer and richly gilded, horseshoe-shaped auditorium, banked high with tiers and able to seat 3,000 music lovers, are being conservatively restored, with the original terracotta floors exhumed from beneath their covering of linoleum. The stage has seen the rise to stardom of singers such as Maria Callas and Luciano Pavarotti. La Scala is due to re-open at the end of 2004; in the meantime, performances are held at the Teatro degli Arcimboldi, zona Bicocca.

Museo Manzoniano

Among the 18th-century *palazzi* on Piazza Belgioioso is the house where the great Romantic novelist Alessandro Manzoni lived for almost 60 years until his death in 1873. The museum is devoted to the author's life, and is filled with his books, pictures and furniture.

Museo Poldi Pezzoli

A stone's throw away on Via Manzoni, this first-rate museum is named after the 19th-century owner of both the *palazzo* and its contents. There are fine displays of Murano glassware, 16th and 17th-century weapons, armour, Meissen and Capodimonte porcelain, clocks, sundials, facemasks and Gobelins tapestries.

The art collection includes a superb polyptych by Cristoforo Moretti, Pollaiolo's 15th-century *Portrait of a Young Woman* and works by Giovanni Bellini, Mantegna, Piero della Francesca, Botticelli, Lorenzo Lotto, Tiepolo and Canaletto.

Pinacoteca di Brera

Further north, on the corner of Via Brera and Via Fiori Oscuri, the Jesuits' 17th-century Brera Palace houses one of Italy's most important collections of paintings. It was founded by Napoleon in 1809, and based on the cultural plunder from both Church and aristocracy. The founder retains a prominent place at the Brera to this day: Antonio Canova's bronze statue of a nude Napoleon stands in the centre of the main courtyard. Beyond it a stone staircase leads up to the gallery.

The Brera has a staggering array of masterpieces. Outstanding are Giovanni Bellini's sensitive *Pietà*, Mantegna's *Cristo* 21

High-flown sculpture embellishes the monumental Stazione Centrale.

Morto, with its famously foreshortened perspective, Tintoretto's *Discovery of the Body of St Mark* and Piero della Francesca's hook-nosed Duke of Urbino, finding his way into a picture of the *Madonna and Child with Angels and Saints*.

A dramatic contrast in Renaissance styles can be observed in two of the gallery's best works: Raphael's highly formal *Marriage of the Madonna*, with its cool, idealized vision of life, at the opposite end of the aesthetic spectrum from Caravaggio's determinedly human, warts-and-all portrayal of Christ's hosts in the chiaroscuro *Supper at Emmaus*.

The Brera also boasts tremendous paintings by Rembrandt, El Greco and Van Dyck, as well as the cold blast of 20th-century experimentalism in Modigliani, Braque, Picasso, de Chirico, Balla and Boccioni.

North of the Centre

A variety of treats are in store for those who venture away from the centre of town. Start in the fashion centre of Italy, move on to a park with an art gallery and a zoo, take in a railway station that's also a famously extravagant example of Fascist architecture, and wind up at a cemetery that's a metropolis in itself.

Via Monte Napoleone

The area of concentrated trendiness bordered by Via Monte Napoleone to the southwest and Via della Spiga to the northeast has the smartest Milanese designs in clothes, shoes, jewellery and furniture. The boutiques here amount to a roll call of the leading names in fashion. The merchandise doesn't come cheap, but it costs nothing, of course, just to wander around and rub shoulders with the Milanese at their most self-consciously cool.

Giardini Pubblici

These public gardens north of Via della Spiga were laid out in the 1780s and landscaped in the popular English style a century later. There's plenty to do for people of all ages, with a zoo, a planetarium, Italy's largest natural history museum, a children's railway, playground and a pedal-car track.

At the entrance to the park is the neoclassical Villa Reale, built for the wealthy Belgioioso family in 1790 and used by Napoleon as his palace during visits to Milan. It now houses the Gallery of Modern Art, with paintings by Picasso, Cézanne, Renoir and Matisse, collections of Italian Impressionist and Futurist paintings, and an important set of sculptures by Mariano Marini.

In the Palazzo Dugnani, a small but enjoyable Cinema Museum displays cameras, projectors, old posters and other film paraphernalia.

Stazione Centrale

Completed in 1931, and covered in grandiose sculptures, Roman-style mosaics and imperial eagles, Milan's main railway station has as much to do with ideology as architecture, and encapsulates Mussolini's obsession with trains as symbolic of national prestige. Like it or loathe it, this is a remarkable building; the vaulted metal and glass roof over the track is superb.

You can contrast the Fascist bombast of its façade with the elegant lines of the post-war Pirelli tower, across the Piazza Duca d'Aosta. This is now the seat of Lombardy's regional government.

Cimitero Monumentale

West of the Central Station, Milan's great necropolis dates from the 1860s, when the newly rich bourgeoisie felt a need to declare their financial success in death as well as life. Graves here are marked by pyramids, obelisks, mini-cathedrals and great marble temples. The centrepiece is Alessandro Manzoni's huge neo-Byzantine monument. Many vie for the title of most flamboyant. But perhaps the most moving is a simple cube framework dedicated

23

to the Milanese who were killed in German concentration camps in World War II.

South of the Centre

The last remains of the Roman city of Mediolanum can be seen around the Porta Ticinese at the southern edge of central Milan, as well as two important ancient churches. A morning's sightseeing can be rounded off with lunch at one of the modish cafés in the face-lifted Navigli canal district.

San Lorenzo Maggiore

Facing a Roman portico of 16 Corinthian columns moved here from a temple in the 4th century, the basilica of San Lorenzo, on the Corso di Porta Ticinese, can claim to be the oldest church in Milan. The 19th-century façade gives way to the octagonal, 4th-century Cappella di Sant'Aquilino, with early Romano-Christian mosaics of Jesus and the Apostles and Elijah in his chariot. The chapel is entered through a Roman door dating from the 1st century AD.

Sant'Eustorgio

At the southern end of the Parco della Basilica, near the medieval Ticinese town gate, the original 4th-century church was built to house the relics of the Three Kings. But in 1162, Frederick Barbarossa sacked Milan, virtu-ally destroyed Sant'Eustorgio and carted the bones off to Cologne cathedral. They were once kept in the large Roman sarcophagus in the Chapel of the Magi.

The church was subsequently rebuilt in Romanesque style, and the apse and tall belltower date from this time. But the highlight is the glorious Portinari Chapel, a masterpiece of early Tuscan Renaissance added in the 1460s and attributed to the Florentine architect Michelozzo Michelozzi. It's dedicated to St Peter Martyr, a Papal Inquisitor who was bludgeoned to death near Lake Como in 1252, and whose magnificent tomb, carved by Giovanni di Balduccio in 1339, stands in the centre of the chapel. The chapel walls are decorated by Vincenzo Foppa's brilliant frescoes of 1468 depicting the life of the saint.

Navigli Canals

Built in 1177 and linking Milan to a whole network of North Italian waterways, the Naviglio Grande Canal area was until the 1950s a bustling port, and as such a rumbustious, working-class district of warehouses, bars and poor housing. A brief stroll by the canal today reveals the transformation that has occurred: modernized apartments beloved of Milan's affluent would-be Bohemians, smart cafés, and the city's best bars and nightlife scene.

Within easy reach of Milan, a number of beautiful old towns flourished in the Middle Ages but were ultimately overshadowed by their giant neighbour. Fortunately, this means that their ancient streets and architectural splendours have often retained their original atmosphere. Today, these towns contain some of Northern Italy's most striking monuments and museums.

Bergamo

About 50 km (30 miles) northeast of Milan, Bergamo is divided between a marvellous medieval upper town (Città Alta) and a more modern lower town (Città Bassa). It was an independent city state in the 12th century, passing into Visconti hands after 1329, and from 1428 became an outpost of the Venetian Empire for more than 350 years.

Città Bassa

From outside the railway station, the Viale Papa Giovanni XXIII propels you into the heart of the Città Bassa. On the large main square, the 18th-century Teatro Donizetti is named after the famous opera composer, born in Bergamo in 1797. Nearby, the San Bartolomeo church has an altar painted in 1516 by Lorenzo Lotto. On the other side of the piazza is the lively café-lined Sentierone area.

Città Alta

Continue past the fascist-era buildings of the Piazza Vittorio Veneto, and along Viale Vittorio Emanuele II to a funicular that takes you up to the Città Alta. Here, in the exquisite Piazza Vecchia, is one of Europe's most pleasing combinations of medieval and Renaissance architecture. The square is dominated by the 12th-century Torre del Comune. Take the lift to the top for great views of the city and surrounding countryside.

The Palazzo della Ragione is marked with a Lion of St Mark, in honour of the city's Venetian past. Pass through its lower arches to the magnificent Piazza del Duomo. It confronts you immediately with the riotously ornamented Renaissance façade of the Colleoni Chapel, dating from the 1470s and designed by Giovanni Amadeo. Bartolomeo Colleoni was an archetypal *condottiere*, an aristocratic mercenary who fought for the Venetians against the Visconti. The interior contains his equestrian tomb and ceiling paintings by Tiepolo.

Next door is the equally remarkable 12th-century Romanesque Basilica of Santa Maria Maggiore. Its sumptuous porch opens to a splendid interior that dazzles the senses, with 16th-century Flemish tapestries, carved choir stalls and superb intarsia-worked Biblical scenes in front of the chancel rail designed by Lorenzo Lotto. At the back of the church is the tomb of Donizetti. A museum devoted to the composer can be found along Via Arena. His birthplace, at Via Borgo Canale 14, also contains a small museum.

Just below the Porta Sant'Agostino gate, the excellent Galleria dell'Accademia Carrara is one of Northern Italy's best art galleries. It contains some especially fine Renaissance portraiture, such as Botticelli's *Giuliano de' Medici* and others by Bellini, Lotto and Pisanello. There are also works by Raphael, Titian, Tintoretto and Mantegna, and non-Italian masters such as Velasquez, Holbein and Brueghel.

Pavia

A mere 35 km (22 miles) south of Milan, Pavia was the original choice of capital by the Lombards. Their kings were crowned here, as later were the emperors Charlemagne and Frederick Barbarossa. Pavia enjoyed an economic and intellectual heyday during the Middle Ages, but by the 13th century it had been subdued by the Milanese counts. The town's distinguished university was founded in 1361, based on a school of jurisprudence that dated back to the 9th century.

Pavia retains its Roman street plan, and revolves around two main intersecting roads, Corso Strada Nuova and Corso Mazzini. At the north end of town, the small 12th-century San Pietro in Ciel d'Oro is mentioned in Dante's *Paradiso*. The church contains the tomb of the Roman poet Boethius in the crypt, and the bones of St Augustine in the magnificent Arca di Sant'Agostino altar, a Gothic masterpiece carved in the 1360s.

To the east, the huge 14th-century Castello Visconteo has a superb arcaded courtyard decorated with terracotta. This houses the Museo Civico, with a collection of Roman and Lombard archaeological finds, and the Pinacoteca, with works by Giovanni Bellini, Foppa, Correggio and Tiepolo.

A short distance south is the main university area, centred around the Piazza Leonardo da Vinci. The square contains three medieval towers and the remains of the 12th-century Sant'Eusebio church. The nearby Bar Bordoni

The charterhouse of Pavia (top). Bergamo landscape (bottom).

27

is a famous student hangout as well as a good spot for some refreshment.

Crossing Strada Nuova, you come to the bustling Piazza della Vittoria, with bars, cafés and a market. At the southern end, the Broletto, Pavia's ancient town hall, is dwarfed by the Duomo behind it. This enormous 15th-century church was worked on by artists of the calibre of Leonardo, Bramante and Amadeo, though even its greatest admirers admit it has a rather unlovely appearance.

From here, head southeast to the city's outstanding Romanesque church, San Michele Maggiore, completed in 1155 on 7th-century Lombard foundations. This is where the Lombard kings and, later, Frederick Barbarossa were crowned. The superb sandstone façade is decorated with sculpted friezes of dragons, griffins and mermaids. Inside there are interesting carved capitals on the columns.

Certosa di Pavia

At the end of a long tree-lined road 10 km (6 miles) north of Pavia, the Certosa, or Charterhouse, ranks among the greatest of Italy's Renaissance buildings. It was commissioned by Gian Galeazzo Visconti in the 1390s as a grandiose family tomb, and he directed many of the same artists and masons to work on it who were already busy on Milan's Duomo. As the centrepiece of a magnificent courtyard, the church's stunning façade certainly reveals a similar spirit. Its multitudinous statuary is positively awesome. The church took so long to construct that by the time it was finished the original Gothic style had been transformed into this Renaissance gem. What you see today is largely the achievement of the great Pavian architect Giovanni Amadeo, who worked on the church for 30 years at the end of the 15th and beginning of the 16th centuries.

Inside, note the vaulted ceiling and huge metalwork screen, beyond which you'll find marvellous inlaid choir stalls and the marble tombs of Ludovico il Moro and his wife Beatrice d'Este. Tucked away in the old sacristy is a superbly carved 15th-century altarpiece, while the tomb of Gian Galeazzo Visconti himself is in the right-hand transept.

A nearby door gives access to the terracotta-decorated Little Cloister, where the Refectory has a *Last Supper* painting, fine ceiling frescoes by Bergognone and an ornately carved pulpit. A passage leads to the magnificent Great Cloister, also with terracotta sculpting, whose great arcaded walkways contain 24 cottage-like monks' cells.

Fanning out to the north and east of Milan, the enchanting mountain lakes of Northern Italy have provided glamorous playgrounds for visitors from far and wide since ancient Roman times. Milanese city-dwellers, lucky to live only an hour or so away, flock here in summer to escape the furnace of the metropolis, while northerners pour across the Alps in search of the perfect combination of natural beauty and relaxed Italian resort life. Every lake has its own particular charm, and it's hard to resist heading off to just one more, to discover new delights. But there's no need to rush. A trip to the lakes can be habit-forming, and you may find you are planning the next visit even before this one is over.

Lake Orta

Tiny Lake Orta is a mere 13 km (9 miles) long and, apart from being the westernmost of the lakes, is the only one to lie entirely in Piedmont. Although its status has been that of a Cinderella in comparison to its bigger and more famous siblings, it has lately become popular with tourists spurning the well-trodden paths of other lakes.

Orta San Giulio

Orta's attractive main town sits on a scenic peninsula jutting into the lake's eastern side, and its cluster of narrow, cobbled lanes mean that cars have to be left outside the centre. The lanes will

MAGICAL ISLAND

Isola San Giulio in Lake Orta was notoriously infested with pests—serpents, dragons and the like—until Giulio arrived in 390 AD. He had been sent by the Church in Rome to convert the heathens who lived in these wild parts. Sizing up the island as the perfect place for a religious teacher to set up shop, he found that the locals refused to row him there. Unperturbed, the world's first windsurfer used his cloak and staff as a means to skim across and chase out the monsters. He founded a sanctuary, rebuilt in the 11th century as a basilica. The church is filled with details showing Giulio's exploits. Look in particular for the great black marble pulpit, with its carvings of San Giulio leaning on his sword, and the 16th-century frescoes by scholars of Gaudenzio Ferrari in the left aisle.

29

inevitably lead you to the Piazza Motta, with its 16th-century town hall, pavement cafés and views of the lake. From the waterfront, you can take a small boat across to Isola San Giulio, with a monastery, 11th-century Romanesque basilica and campanile.

Back on the mainland, above the town is the Sacro Monte. Climb up through the beech trees to its 20 chapels dating mainly from the early 17th century, each with lifesize terracotta statues and frescoes reflecting the life of St Francis of Assisi. Even better is the splendid view of the lake and Isola San Giulio.

Pettenasco

To the north of Orta San Giulio, this peaceful village has a delightful lakefront and is a great place for avoiding the stresses and strains of modern life. Just up the coast is the Punta di Crabbia, a headland with a view that covers virtually the entire lake.

In the hills behind the town, Armeno and Ameno are both pleasant spots centred around fine old churches. At nearby Vacciago, the villa of artist Antonio Calderara, who died in 1978, displays his work as well as other modern paintings and sculptures which he owned.

Around the Lake

On the northwest side of the lake, the village of Quarna Sotto is known for the manufacture of musical instruments, and has an interesting museum devoted to them.

Further south, San Maurizio d'Opaglio is the centre of Italy's tap-making industry. You can find out more at the undoubtedly unique Museo del Rubinetto. Above the town, the Santuario della Madonna del Sasso has 18th-century frescoes and panoramic views across to Orta San Giulio.

Lake Maggiore

Called Lacus Verbanus by the Romans because of the verbena growing around it, Lake Mag-

THE THREE BEST LAKE ISLANDS Isola San Giulio, in Lake Orta, has an 11th-century church and a legend that the island was once infested by dragons. An exotic garden and an art-crammed *palazzo* are packed onto the Borromeo-owned **Isola Bella**, on Lake Maggiore. Tiny Lake Iseo can boast Italy's biggest lake island, **Monte Isola**.

giore zigzags for 63 km (39 miles) into the mountains, its northern end jutting well into Switzerland. The lake is dotted with charming villages and attractive resorts; terraced gardens blooming with azaleas, camellias and rhododendrons drop down to the blue waters. It has been a stronghold and retreat of the famous Borromeo family for centuries, and they still own the Borromean Islands, which are not to be missed.

Arona

This was the birthplace of St Charles Borromeo, and on a hill above the town, there's a colossal copper statue of him, 23 m (75 ft) high, that can be seen from the other side of the lake. Completed in 1698, it's hollow with a vertiginous spiral staircase leading to the top, where you can literally get inside the head of a saint.

Meina

A short distance to the north, this pretty village became a popular resort for the wealthy during the 18th century, when its elegant neoclassical villas, such as the handsome Villa Feraggiana, were built. From here you can head up to Massino Visconti, the 12th-century home of the Visconti family before their ambition took them off to become the Dukes of Milan.

Belgirate

A small, attractive little town 5 km (3 miles) up from Meina, it derives a certain fame from the fact that the patriot Giuseppe Garibaldi vacationed here at the Villa Bono Cairoli. There's also a nice main piazza and Santa Marta church, decorated with 15th-century frescoes.

Stresa

The most favoured of all the lake resorts, this appealing town is set amid luxuriant vegetation, with a fine lakeside promenade overlooking the Borromean Islands. In 1935 it was the meeting place of British, French and Italian statesmen, who notably failed to make a stand against Hitler's rearming of Germany. It's still popular for staging conferences and major events like the Settimane Musicali di Stresa, an international music festival held each year in late August and early September.

Piazza Cadorna is the café-lined centre of town, but the lakeside promenade is its real glory. Break off from your stroll for a drink at the luxurious Grand Hotel des Iles Borromées, used by Ernest Hemingway as a setting for *A Farewell to Arms*. You might then want to visit the gardens of one of the impressive lakeside villas, such as the Villa Pallavicino, or make your way to 31

The perfect hideaway: Isola dei Pescatori, smallest of the Borromean Islands.

the Stresa Lido, from which a funicular ascends Monte Mottarone. The exhilarating view from its peak, 1,491 m (4,892 ft), takes in all of the Lombardy lakes and the Alps. A panoramic road (toll after Alpino) climbs the mountain; past Gignese, at Alpino, you can visit the Giardino Alpinia, displaying more than 2,000 varieties of mountain plants.

Borromean Islands

Reached by boat from Stresa and Baveno, these lumps of once-barren rock were transformed by the Borromeo family into baroque gems of fine *palazzi* and splendid gardens.

On Isola Bella, the formal terraced gardens of sweet-scented plants, grottoes and statues were the brainchild of Count Carlo III Borromeo, who had the soil ferried over from the mainland. Work began around 1630 under the architect Angelo Crivelli. The project was an extravagant present for Carlo's wife Isabella (after whom the island was named). The baroque Palazzo Borromeo came later, and is richly furnished with paintings by Giordano and Tiepolo, 16th-century Flemish tapestries and an 18th-century puppet theatre.

Isola dei Pescatori is in complete contrast to the Borromean grandeur of its neighbour, with a quiet, picturesque village and little else.

The third island, Isola Madre, boasts a 16th-century villa set among palms and ancient cypresses. The botanical garden also has fine displays of camellias and azaleas, and is patrolled by peacocks and pheasants.

Baveno

Though it's quieter than Stresa these days, Baveno pre-dates it as a fashionable resort, hitting the headlines in 1879 when Queen Victoria stayed at the Castello Branca.

The town has some interesting buildings, including the 12th-century Romanesque San Gervasio e Protasio church and campanile. Next door is an octagonal Renaissance baptistery, with 15th-century frescoes on the ceiling, and in front there's a colonnaded cloister with frescoes dating from a century later.

A turn-off on the Verbania road leads to the minute but delightful Lago di Mergozzo, perfect for swimming in summer.

Verbania

Verbania was formed out of three towns, Suna, Pallanza and Intra, in 1939. The lakeside at Pallanza is lined with bars, hotels and *gelaterias*. Inland, the Museo del Paesaggio, with an appealing range of 19th- and 20th-century landscape paintings of Lake Maggiore, is located in the 16th-century Palazzo Viani-Dugnani.

Further along the waterfront, Verbania's star attraction is the Villa Taranto. It was bought in 1931 by a retired Scottish soldier, Captain Neil McEachern, who made full use of the exceptionally mild winter climate to create one of the world's great botanical gardens. More than 20,000 varieties of exotic plants thrive in its 16 ha (40 acres), including *Victoria amazonica*, giant waterlilies from Brazil, and Japanese maples, all of which have acclimatized to this spot just below the Alps. The gardens are open from April to October.

Ghiffa

At the end of a string of small villages, Ghiffa is a charming town of villas, gardens and a pleasant waterfront promenade. From the promontory you can probably enjoy the most complete panoramic view of this meandering lake.

Up from the town, the Santuario della Trinità has three chapels dating from the 17th century.

To Cannobio

As you approach Cannero Riviera, the mountains close in dramatically. The islands just offshore might have come straight out of the pages of a Gothic novel. They 33 were once the stronghold of a family of bloodthirsty brigands, who were finally beaten by Filippo Visconti in 1414. The scenic ruins you can see today are the remains of a later castle built by the Borromeos.

Not far from the Swiss border, Cannobio is an atmospheric medieval town with a maze of narrow alleyways criss-crossing a steep hill. If you're there on a Sunday, you can look around the lively market held on the waterfront piazza. Nearby, the Santuario della Pietà was built to house a miraculous picture of the Dead Christ, said to have shed real blood in the 16th century. It's now part of Defendente Ferrari's splendid altarpiece.

From Cannobio, you can drive across the frontier to the Swiss resorts of Ascona and Locarno (don't forget your passport).

Santa Caterina del Sasso

The Lombardy side of the lake is not as packed with eye-catching resorts. But one place which is definitely worth seeing is Santa Caterina del Sasso, a Carmelite convent clinging to a rockface that overhangs the lake. Further south, Angera is dominated by a one of the best castles in Northern Italy, the Rocca. In a strategically vital position, it was held by the Lombards, the Torrianis and the Viscontis, until in 1449 the Bor-

romeos took control—and they have remained in possession to this day.

Lake Lugano

Also known by the Italians as Lago di Ceresio, this narrow, wriggly lake lies mainly in Switzerland, but the northeastern and southwestern branches burrow into Italy, and on the east bank is the tiny Italian enclave of Campione d'Italia.

Lugano

The Swiss seized most of the lake from Milan in 1512, and in so doing acquired one of their loveliest towns, which lies winsomely around the bay below cone-shaped Monte San Salvatore and Monte Brè. Its best man-made feature, though, is pure Italian Renaissance: the church of Santa Maria degli Angioli on the western shore. Dating from 1510, the church's magnificent frescoes were painted by Leonardo's pupil Bernardino Luini, and the huge *Crucifixion* is thought by some to rival works of the master himself.

Besides its elegant shopping streets and first-rate restaurants, Lugano boasts a couple of interesting museums. The Museo Cantonale d'Arte has works by Degas and Renoir, while out at the Villa Favorita, on the road to Castagnola, the Thyssen-Bornemisza collection of modern European and American art is on display. The family's more famous collection of Old Masters is now in Spain.

For great views of the city and lake, take the funicular, either up Monte San Salvatore from the suburb of Paradiso, or to the top of Monte Brè from Cassarate.

Porlezza

Back in Italy, Porlezza, at the east end of the lake, is a pleasant town that always seems Italian to those arriving from Switzerland, and rather Swiss to those used to the full-blooded ways of Italy. The town was noted for producing artists during the Renaissance, including Guglielmo della Porta, one of Michelangelo's favourite pupils. Today, it's an enjoyable place simply to wander around and savour the relaxed atmosphere. The mountain country beyond Porlezza is breathtaking.

Head for the village of Seghebbia for an alpine walk along a ridge to Monte Garzirola, or to Cavargna for access to the remote Lepontine Alps.

Campione d'Italia

An intriguing anomaly, this little piece of Italy immediately across the lake from Lugano is surrounded entirely by Switzerland. The village was bequeathed by its owner to the Sant'Ambrogio church in Milan in the 8th century, and its history has been tied to it ever since.

Once famed for its master masons who went out to build many of Northern Italy's greatest churches, Campione's reputation as a resort now rests entirely on the grand Casinò Municipale, which began operating during World War I and brings bucketloads of Swiss francs to fill the region's coffers.

4

THE FOUR BEST VILLAS The 18th-century **Villa Carlotta** on Lake Como has a collection of Canova sculptures and offers great views from its terraced gardens. Also on Como, **Villa Serbelloni**, in Bellagio, has spectacular grounds with camellias, magnolias and rose trees. **Villa Taranto**, on Lake Maggiore, is renowned for the 20,000 different exotic plants from around the world in its remarkable botanical gardens. Gabriele d'Annunzio's villa, **Il Vittoriale**, overlooking Lake Garda, is a bizarre mixture of museum and shrine dedicated to modern Italy's most famous poet.

Lake Como

Of all the lakes, this one caused the greatest passion in Romantics writers such as Wordsworth and Shelley, who found poetic inspiration in its dramatic scenery. Spurs of the surrounding mountains plunge sheer into the cobalt waters. The grey-green and silver of olive trees alternate with mulberry, chestnut, figs and oleander. Grim-visaged castles tower above tiny flowered villages and harbours.

Como is the deepest lake in Europe, reaching up to 410 m (1,345 ft) in depth. The glacier that created it clearly hit an obstacle at the place where Bellagio now lies, separating to create the two distinctive legs. At the toe of the left leg is the lake's biggest city, which shares its evocative name.

Como

Home to major silk and textile industries, and with a population approaching 100,000, this is not so much a resort as an important regional centre. It has had a long and proud history. Used by the Romans both as a strategic point on the road to the Alps and as a holiday destination, it rose to prominence as one of the wealthy city-states that rivalled—and warred with—Milan in the Middle Ages. The city has had more than its share of famous sons. The Roman writers Pliny the Elder and his nephew, the Younger, were both born in Como, as was the physicist Alessandro Volta, who developed the first electric battery and whose name has survived as "volt".

Statues of the two pre-Christian Plinys are placed somewhat incongruously among the saints on the white marble façade of the splendid 14th-century Duomo. The baroque dome was added to this Gothic-Renaissance edifice by the architect Filippo Juvarra in 1744. Inside the cathedral, you can admire 16th-century tapestries in the nave, and paintings by Bernardino Luini and Gaudenzio Ferrari.

Next door, the red, white and grey striped marble Broletto, or town hall, dates from 1215.

A short way north, the wide Piazza Cavour is Como's pulsing heart, packed with hotels and cafés, thronged with people and open to views of the lake. By the lake to the west, the Giardini Pubblici contains the Tempio Volta, a neoclassical temple honouring the great, self-educated scientist and housing a small museum of his instruments.

Cernobbio

Not far to the north, this busy town is best known for the sumptuous Villa d'Este. Built in 1557 for Como-born Cardinal Gallio, the Papal Secretary of State, it was later occupied by Caroline of Brunswick, who came here to avoid the publicity following her estrangement from George IV, and to carry on her energetic social life in style. Since 1873, it has been one of Europe's premiere luxury hotels.

A road winds upwards from Cernobbio to Monte Bisbino, 1,325 m (4,347 ft), with stunning views of the lake.

Moltrasio

There are more excellent villas in this small resort, built on the lakeside slope of Monte Bisbino and cut in two by a scenic ravine. The 18th-century Villa Passalacqua has a delightful garden that's open to the public; the Villa Salterio played host to the composer Bellini in 1831. The town also has an 11th-century Romanesque church and belltower.

Tremezzo

Many of Tremezzo's stately villas have been turned into hotels, but the best-known villa on the entire lake remains gloriously intact. Set in magnificent terraced gardens filled with camellias, azaleas and rhododendrons, and approached by a shady avenue of plane trees known as the Via del Paradiso, the Villa Carlotta is a marvel of 18th-century aristocratic style.

Originally owned by the Clerici family, its name was changed in the 1850s when it was given by a Prussian princess to her daughter Carlotta as a wedding gift. The cool interior retains its neoclassical ornamentation, with period paintings and plasterwork, and a number of Antonio Canova's sculptures on display.

Cadenabbia

Cadenabbia became extremely popular with English tourists in the 19th century and has an Anglican church from that time. The lake is at its widest here, and from the shore you can see across to where it splits at Bellagio. The view is even better from the 16th-century church of San Martino high above the town.

Menaggio

With easy access from Lugano, this elegant resort provides a popular weekend break for visitors from Switzerland. There are plenty of stylish shops and a profusion of fine hotels and restaurants, while the attractive harbour is a magnet for artists. A frequent ferry service crosses to Varenna on the eastern side.

Menaggio also has a reputation for its sporting life; there are tennis courts, an 18-hole golf course and some of the best hiking in the region to be had in the mountains above the town, culminating in such peaks as Monte Bregagno, more than 2,000 m (6,500 ft) high.

Musso

About 16 km (10 miles) north of Menaggio, you come to Musso. In the 16th century its castle had a notorious inhabitant known as Il Medeghino. This petty adventurer and member of the Medici family terrorized the inhabitants of the lake shores with the connivance of the Sforzas in Milan. Later he went to fight in the Netherlands for Emperor Charles V and ended up with the title of Viceroy of Bohemia. His tomb is in Milan cathedral.

Dongo

This is where Italian partisans caught Mussolini and his mistress Clara Petacci on April 27, 1945, as they tried to flee to Switzerland in a German lorry. Both were shot the next day a few miles to the south. In the 13th century, Dongo and the neighbouring villages of Sorico and Gravedona founded a short-lived republic known as the Tre Pievi, the Three Parishes. Gravedona has a charming grey-and-white striped 12th-century Romanesque church.

Varenna

Returning down the eastern shore of the lake, take a side road round an inlet to see the Romanesque Abbey of Piona, with its superb cloister added in 1257.

Como's main east shore town is an important stop for boats to Menaggio, Bellagio and Cadenabbia. The town has some great medieval buildings, not least the 10th-century Oratorio di San Giovanni and the Romanesque San Giorgio, with a huge fresco of St Christopher on the exterior. Villa Monastero was built in 1208 for Cistercian nuns. Bird-lovers will enjoy the Ornithological Museum in Villa Venini, which concentrates on the extensive range of Como's birdlife.

Above Varenna, there's a 7th-century castello, thought to have been the home of the Lombard Queen Theodolinda; while south of the town at Fiumelatte is a real curiosity—Italy's shortest river. At 250 m (820 ft), "milk river" as the name translates, is a torrent of white water that bursts out of the rocks in spring and stops in autumn. Leonardo da Vinci was puzzled by it, but never found its source.

Lecco

The eastern leg of Lake Como is known as Lago di Lecco. Lecco itself is a small industrial town at the southern tip of the lake. It was the childhood home of the novelist Alessandro Manzoni, and the setting for his masterpiece, *The Betrothed*. Villa Manzoni, his former house, is now a museum, and there's a large monument to the author in the middle of town.

Bellagio

The best and most direct route from Varenna to Bellagio is by ferry. The "Pearl of the Lake" is perfectly situated on a promontory where the two legs meet; there are great views from all over town of both lake and mountains. The busy waterfront is a delightful place to stop for a drink and take in the scene. Medieval streets lead up from here to the 11th-century San Giacomo church, with a painting in the sacristy by Vincenzo Foppa, and the 18th-century Villa Serbelloni, with a famously beautiful Italianate garden. Inland from Bellagio, there are unrivalled vistas of the whole lake from on top of Monte San Primo, reached from the road to Valassina.

Torno

Torno is on the lake's western leg, towards Como from Bellagio. Here, built right against the lake, the Villa Pliniana dates from 1570 and is chiefly known for the high quality of its guest list, which at various times included Shelley, Byron, Stendhal and Rossini. In the garden is an intermittent waterfall that was mentioned as a curiosity by both Plinys, hence the villa's name.

Lake Iseo

Only 25 km (15 miles) in length, Iseo is the smallest of the five main lakes, but it makes up for this in terms of charm, and also by managing to contain Italy's largest lake island. Clad in vineyards, orchards and olive trees, Monte Isola—"Mountain Island"—rises to 600 m (1,968 ft), and has hotels and a campsite.

At the southwest corner of the lake, Sarnico is a major ferry terminus. It's also well-known in the speed-boat world, with an important manufacturing industry based here and international races held just offshore. The town has an attractive mixture of old buildings and Art Nouveau villas, as well as the 15th-century church of San Paolo.

To the north of here, the Santuario di Dossa looms high above the village of Tavernola Bergamasca. Its 15th-century church contains interesting frescoes, and legend has it the superb views of Lake Iseo were used by Leonardo as the backdrop to his *Mona Lisa*.

Located at the lake's northern end, Lovere is a small industrial town with a beautifully frescoed Renaissance church, Santa Maria in Valvendra; and in the neoclassical Galleria dell'Accademia Tadini, a surprisingly good art collection which includes works by Jacopo Bellini, Tiepolo and Magnasco.

Lake Iseo can boast some fantastic natural wonders apart from Monte Isola. On the eastern side, take the winding road up from Marone to the mountain village of Zone. At Cislano there's a good view of the amazing *piramidi di erosione*, a range of massive rock pyramids, many of whose pointed peaks are topped by large boulders.

From the lake's northern town of Pisogne, you can head up into the Val Camonica, where the national park near Capo di Ponte has rock carvings dating back 8,000 years.

Lake Idro

The cold waters of this crystalline mountain lake will deter all but the hardiest swimmers, and are probably enjoyed more by anglers, who come here for the trout fishing. The lake is long and narrow and the mountains seem to erupt straight out of the water.

Idro, at the lake's southernmost point, is a small, pleasant village. Anfo, on the southwest shore, is built on a set of steep terraces. There's an attractive church, with a 12th-century belltower and Renaissance frescoes, and the 15th-century castle, Rocca d'Anfo, where Garibaldi set up his headquarters in 1866.

The delightful town of Bagolino stands some way back from the lake. There's a traditional carnival here, plus the church of San Rocco, with important 15th-century frescoes by Giovanni da Cemmo.

Lake Ledro

Little Lake Ledro is beautifully situated in the mountains, not far from the northwest side of Lake Garda, and can boast decent beaches and a quiet, away-from-it-all atmosphere that's sometimes hard to find in its noisier neighbours.

At the eastern end of the lake, Molina di Ledro is a pleasant town that has become known for the prehistoric lake dwellings discovered here in 1929. They proved to be part of a major Bronze Age settlement. The interesting Museo delle Palafitte displays relics from the excavations, such as axes, pottery and jewellery, as well as a reconstruction of a lake dwelling.

With plenty of sporting activities on offer, the lake's main resort is at Pieve di Ledro, at the opposite end to Molina.

Lake Garda

Italy's biggest lake is almost due east of Milan. It stretches for more than 50 km (32 miles), gradually tapering from the bulbous southern shore to its tip at the foot of the Dolomites. Garda's water is especially clean, and very popular with sailing enthusi-

Whatever your pleasure—sporting, literary, gastronomical—you'll be well served at Lake Garda.

asts, windsurfers and waterskiers. The temperate climate supports olive groves, lemon trees, cedars and vineyards, most notably around the Bardolino area.

The Romans adored the lake, and its beauties were sung by Virgil, Horace and Catullus. Nearly 2,000 years later, the wild man of Italian literature, Gabriele d'Annunzio, set up his extraordinary house high above the lake near Gardone Riviera, a sight not to be missed.

Sirmione

Located at the end of a narrow peninsula that thrusts into the foot of the lake, this historic town of little piazzas and great all-round views is entered by a small bridge and ancient gateway. Immediately to the right, the multi-turreted Rocca Scaligera dominates the town. The castle was built in the 13th century by the Scaligeri family from Verona. Local tradition says that they entertained Dante here as a guest.

You can get around Sirmione via the scenic *passeggiata panoramica*, starting at Santa Maria Maggiore, a 15th-century church that is as battlemented as a castle. The central hump of the headland is crested with a superb range of cypresses, while at the tip, set among olive trees and hedges of 41 rosemary, is the fascinating Grotte di Catullo. Despite their name, these 1st-century BC ruins of an immense Roman villa probably had nothing to do with the poet Catullus, although he certainly stayed in these parts. But they provide a vivid picture of how luxurious a lifestyle the Roman elite enjoyed.

Desenzano del Garda

Following the Gardesana Occidentale, the road along the western shore, you soon reach the lake's largest town. Its lively waterfront scene is best taken in from one of the many popular lakeside cafés or restaurants. Just back from the lake, the baroque church of Santa Maria Maddalena has an unusual version of *The Last Supper* by Tiepolo, a rather crowded-looking scene which also includes a serving wench and a dog. A couple of streets away on Via Crocifisso 22, there's an excavated 3rd-century Roman villa, with fine mosaic floors in remarkably good condition.

Salò

Continuing around to the western shore you arrive at this town of narrow old streets by an attractive bay. In 1943 it became the capital of the egregious Republic of Salò, a puppet regime set up by Mussolini under the Germans

---

FUMING IN FIUME

Far larger than life, Gabriele d'Annunzio (1863–1938) was famous in the late 19th century as a writer of passionate and sensuous poetry. Just as his fame was going off the boil, World War I began, providing him with a vast stage on which he could act out the role of Romantic hero. He sought out dangerous assignments, lost an eye in combat when he was with the airforce, and capped it all just after the war with his own private invasion of the Adriatic port of Fiume (Rijeka).

The town had been promised to Italy during the war, but it was given to the newly created Yugoslav state under the Treaty of Versailles. In 1919, d'Annunzio together with 9000 volunteers marched into Fiume, and the poet-conquistador ruled it as a dictator for a year. The Italian government eventually forced him to leave, but the port remained in Italian hands. D'Annunzio's actions made him a hero in Italy, especially to the Nationalists. And the lesson of what one daring and determined man backed up by disciples in black shirts could achieve wasn't lost on d'Annunzio's admirer, Benito Mussolini—with consequences that Italy would come to regret.

after they had rescued him from detention in the Abruzzi mountains. You can learn more about the short-lived republic and other aspects of Italian military history in the Museo del Nastro Azzurro on Via Fantoni.

Gardone Riviera
The marvellous old villas, gardens and fashionable hotels along the lakeside of this splendid resort north of Salò speak eloquently of its rise at the end of the 19th century. The catalyst was a Professor Rohden from Germany, who pointed out the uncommonly temperate climate of this sheltered part of the lake. Be sure to take a stroll around the Hruska Botanical Gardens, with thousands of exotic plants and flowers, where you will see proof positive of the professor's theory.

Il Vittoriale
On a hillside near the Gardone stands a villa almost as flamboyant as the man who lived here, the poet Gabriele d'Annunzio. A nationalist hero and major influence on the Fascist movement, he was given the villa by Mussolini in 1925. Soon disillusioned by the new Italy, however, he retired to Lake Garda to create this extravagant shrine to himself.

The result is part kitsch, part study in morbid self-obsession, but it's never less than fascinating. A World War I biplane, in which d'Annunzio flew over Vienna dropping propaganda leaflets, hangs from the ceiling of the museum; two of the cars which he somewhat ostentatiously drove to the battlefield are on display in the main courtyard. A tour of the house, which is kept in the same semi-darkness that d'Annunzio favoured, reveals a bibliophile with a taste for the macabre. Among an enormous collection of books is the coffin he used for meditating in, an Austrian machine gun, and the shell of his pet turtle, which died from overeating. D'Annunzio had it set in bronze and kept on the dining table as a warning to his guests not to over-indulge.

His mausoleum is on the highest point of the grounds, encircled by the tombs of his disciples and looking out to the lake and the mountains.

Below it is his wildest gesture. The prow of the battleship *Puglia*, captured by d'Annunzio during his 1919 exploit in Fiume, was hauled up to Il Vittoriale where it juts bizarrely out of the hillside.

Riva del Garda
North of Gardone, the mountains grow steeper and terraces of olive trees cling to the slopes. Luxury villas and gardens line the shore, and the air is heavy with the scent 43

of lemon trees *(limoni)*—it's said that the first lemon tree in Europe was grown at the pleasant village of Limone sul Garda. Along this shore the mountains drop so steeply into the water that the road constantly disappears into tunnels before reaching Riva del Garda at the head of the lake. If the little town has a Germanic feel to it, it's probably because it belonged to Austria till 1918. Above it stands a 16th century tower, Il Bastione, a symbol of the Venetian power that once dominated the region.

In the 15th century, the lake was a battleground for fleets of Venetians and Milanese. The Venetians are claimed to have launched 30 ships at Torbole, dragged by oxen over the mountains to surprise the Visconti fleet. Nowadays the bay of Torbole is particularly favoured by windsurfers and sailing enthusiasts.

Malcesine and Beyond

On the lake's eastern shore, Malcesine is a picturesque maze of medieval streets sheltering beneath the 13th-century Castello Scaligero, built by the same family responsible for the fortress in Sirmione. From here you can take a cable car up to Monte Baldo, a popular ski resort, for great views of Garda and the Alps.

Torri del Benaco, once the chief town on this side of the lake, has another 14th-century Scaliger castle, which now serves as a museum on the local culture, covering such subjects as citrus-growing and olive-oil production.

To the south, Punta San Vigilio provides a scenic viewing place where the lake widens out. Surrounded by ancient cypresses, the tiny old church of San Vigilio and the imposing Villa Guarienti overlook the bay.

Garda and southwards

The town of Garda lies in an area that has been inhabited since the Stone Age. Prehistoric caves and remnants of lake dwellings have been found here, and the first town was built by the Romans. The ruined Rocca (castle) above the town belonged to the 10th-century King Berengar II. He is said to have imprisoned a young woman here named Adelaide, after murdering her husband and then trying to marry her off to his son. She escaped and married the German King Otto I instead.

The vineyards south of Garda are home to the famous Bardolino wine. Sipping a glass of the local *vino* outside a café in the main square of the town itself is a simple pleasure to be savoured. Bardolino also boasts two ancient churches, the 8th-century San Zeno and the Romanesque San Severo. On Via Costabella there's a Museo del Vino.

Past Cisano, with its museum devoted entirely to the delights of olive oil (the area here is called the Olive Riviera), you come to Lazise, an attractive fishing village enclosed by 11th-century walls. This was one of the Venetian Republic's main harbours during its wars with Milan. There's a Scaliger castle here too, incorporating a 9th-century Magyar fortress.

Not far from the town, Gardaland is the Italian answer to Disneyworld, a large-scale theme park cum funfair that will keep the children entertained.

Back at the southern end of the lake, Peschiera has massive fortifications dating from Venetian times and strengthened by the Austrians and Napoleon. There's also a fine arched bridge over the Mincio river. About 8 km (5 miles) to the south, Villa Sigurtà has vast spreading gardens renowned for their loveliness.

Lake Levico

Located in the Val Sugana, a narrow valley northeast of Lake Garda, Levico is a minuscule lake that's famed for its pure water and clean air. It's especially popular with Venetians, who race up here for weekend breaks along a direct road from Venice. The main resort, Levico Terme, is situated on the south side of the lake.

The valley itself is richly agricultural, filled with vineyards and orchards, while a stone's throw away is another attractive lake, the Lago di Caldonazzo. For those who seek good Trentino cuisine, local wines and peace and quiet all served up with a garnish of Alpine beauty, this is a must.

THE FIVE BEST VISTAS From the roof of Milan's **Duomo** you can look down on the whole city, and as far as the Alps and the Appennines. At **Orta San Giulio**, on Lake Orta, there's a magical view of the lake island and the church of Madonna del Sasso high up on the opposite shore. Seven of the lakes are visible from the peak of the mighty **Mottarone**, behind Stresa on Lake Maggiore. The **Santuario di Dossa** offers a fine panorama over Lake Iseo, whose rocky scenery is said to have inspired the background to Leonardo's *Mona Lisa*. A supreme vista of Lake Como can be enjoyed from the top of **Monte San Primo**, behind Bellagio.

45

Cultural Notes

Architecture of Scale

Milan might not be blessed with an abundance of great architecture, but it has been uncommonly successful at capturing the essence of the age with just one grand gesture. In the 14th century, Gian Galeazzo Visconti's decision to build the mighty Duomo was a declaration in stone of Milanese self-confidence. The following century it was the Sforzas' turn to make their mark, employing some of Italy's finest Renaissance artists to build the red-brick Castello. Nowhere is there a more spectacular tribute to the 19th-century love of commerce than the monumental Galleria Vittorio Emanuele shopping arcade. The false dawn of the Fascist era is encapsulated in the overpowering bombast of the Stazione Centrale. Post-war modernism hasn't always served the city well, but the elegant lines of the 1960 Pirelli Building, Italy's first skyscraper, express the city's clear-headed optimism for the future.

Leaders of Fashion

Each year, the fashion shows in the *quadrilatero d'oro*—the golden square—of Milan's Monte Napoleone area confirm the city's reputation as the centre of world fashion. London may be avant garde and Paris arty, but the canny Milanese produce marvellously stylish clothes that people actually want to wear. Milan's expertise is based on a centuries-old tradition of style: the word "milliner", meaning "from Milan", dates back to the 16th century, when the fanciest hats, gloves, and even cutlery came from the city. Since the end of World War II, Milan has carefully planned its rise to power in the fashion and design industries, and it has paid off. In an increasingly competitive market, Milan's better transport and business links with the outside world have attracted cutting-edge designers from other Italian cities such as Florence. Today, the city salons no longer exhibit just the latest in clothing. The Salone del Mobile is an event dedicated to furniture; there are exhibitions of home and office design; and the Triennale is a massive decorative arts show held every three years in the 1930s Palazzo dell'Arte.

Leonardo's Milan

A Tuscan by birth, but Milanese by choice, Leonardo came to the city in 1482 at the age of 30 to work for the Duke of Milan as musician, engineer, designer of court festivals and anything else that his capacious mind alighted on. He was also, as he added in his job application, rather handy with a paintbrush. Scholars have speculated as to why he wanted to leave the artistic hotbed of Florence at such a crucial stage in his career, but it's probable that the dazzling Sforza court, and the free rein that would be given to his imagination there, was too tempting to resist. Leonardo spent 24 years in the city, and it was here that his full genius flowered. The *Mona Lisa* (now in the Louvre), the *Last Supper*, at the Santa Maria delle Grazie church, and the classic Renaissance *Portrait of a Musician*, on display in the Pinacoteca Ambrosiana, were all painted during the Milan years. He also developed engineering schemes for digging Milan's canals, and in his notebooks dreamed up countless inventions for everything from flying machines to tanks.

Alessandro Manzoni

Born in Milan in 1785, the novelist is revered throughout Italy for his classic *I promessi sposi* (The Betrothed). Set against the tumultuous backdrop of early 17th-century Lombardy, the novel tells of the struggles of two peasant lovers, Renzo and Lucia, threatened by an aristocratic tyrant and let down by the weakness of their priest. This daringly democratic use of ordinary people in the role of hero and heroine was coupled with a new, accessible prose style that cut through the linguistic barrier of Italy's multitude of dialects. Manzoni's novel was a sensation when

it was first published in 1827. It was immediately taken up by the nationalist Risorgimento movement as a book that summed up their hopes for a modern, unified nation. After Lombardy joined the Italian kingdom in 1859, Manzoni was made a senator, and by the time of his death in 1873, he was one of the most respected figures of his age. His temple-like tomb in Milan's Cimitero Monumentale is the city's grandiose memorial.

San Siro

It's no exaggeration to say that football ranks along with food, fashion and business as the driving force behind Milan's sense of self. The city is home to not just one, but two of the world's most sophisticated teams, Inter and A.C. Milan. To witness the ultimate monument to this, head out to the Lotto metro station any Sunday during the season, and follow the river of fans to San Siro (officially Stadio Giuseppe Meazza). In Piero Pirelli's magnificent 1920s structure, the humble football ground has been raised to a spectacular modernist cathedral of concrete, metal and glass. Almost 90,000 people can congregate to experience the extraordinary mixture of religious fervour and grand theatre that is Italian football. The ground is even more lavish these days. San Siro's facelift for the 1990 World Cup cost an impressive $75 million.

Shopping

From Giorgio Armani to Ermenegildo Zegna, Milan is the A–Z of the fashion world. A truly dazzling range of chic boutiques and designer clothes shops cater to the Milanese effortless sense of style. The prices are to match, of course, so it's fortunate that plenty of other locally made items are available both in the city and around the lakes—more affordable, but all with the same Italian hallmark of style and quality.

Where?

The geographical *capo dei capi* of Italian fashion revolves around the world-famous Via Monte Napoleone, northeast of the Duomo. The area contains the city's best jewellery and antique shops, too. Excellent clothes, food and designer household goods can also be found in stores in the Galleria Vittorio Emanuele, Corso Vittorio Emanuele and Corso Venezia. Street markets offer a less wallet-busting experience, with a Saturday flea market in Viale Gabriele d'Annunzio, and an enjoyably rumbustious one held on the last Sunday of each month along the Naviglio Grande canal.

Away from Milan, the resorts around Lake Maggiore are the places to find excellent ceramic handicrafts; those on Lake Garda are known for gold jewellery, locally made wine and olive oil. Superbly carved woodwork and items made from silk are easy to find in the towns along Lake Como.

What?

Dressing is an art in Milan, and men's and women's clothing purchased here will make you—or your loved one—feel like a million dollars. On top of their wonderful designer suits and dresses, the maestros of Monte Napoleone turn out the finest in shoes, leather items, lingerie, swimwear and children's clothing.

Pride in the quality of design permeates far and wide. Look for kitchenware—such as futuristic espresso machines, modernistic toasters and pasta makers—and other household gadgets that would look equally at home in a gallery of modern art.

In a country awash with art and antiques, it's no surprise that the old furniture, paintings and jew-

When you're shopping in the Galleria Vittorio Emanuele, take time to admire the architecture.

ellery that reach the markets are fabulous, although they are rarely at bargain prices. You might not be able to take your favourite painting home with you, but Italian art books are lavish showcases for the stunning array of art in the galleries and museums, and make fine gifts.

Italian craftsmanship is second-to-none. Ceramics, glassware and jewellery are all worth seeking out.

Gourmet gifts

When foreigners think of Italy, its food and wine are likely to come to mind as easily as its art treasures, and with good reason.

Probably the most irresistible urge to buy will occur among the sweet shops and wine sellers. *Panettone*, a deliciously light brioche, studded with raisins and candied fruit, originated in Milan around 1490. It is generally on sale around Christmas time. Cheeses from around Italy can be found here, but for travelling it's probably best to stick to the hard variety such as Parmesan (from nearby Parma), which can be bought in huge chunks. Ideal offerings also include biscuits, chocolates, nougat *(torrone)*, packets of designer pasta and local olive oil and wine, such as Bardolino from Lake Garda.

49

Dining Out

Milanese restaurants are as bustling and cosmopolitan as the city itself, but it is Italian cuisine that provides the richest flavour, and the regional specialities alone will satisfy the most demanding palate. Colourful trattorias always manage to serve good quality pasta and pizza; more upmarket restaurants provide traditional dishes spruced up for exacting modern tastes.

Prima Colazione

If possible, skip the hotel breakfast for a *prima colazione* at any of the small local cafés. In Milan, kickstart the day with a *briosche* (a type of sweet croissant) and *cappuccino* in the frenetic company of the city's money-makers.

Antipasti

Classic starters are *affettati misti*, slices of salami, ham, coppa and pancetta, and, in season, *prosciutto con melone*, juicy melon served with wafer-thin slices of Parma or San Daniele ham. Or try the *carciofi alla milanese*, artichokes served with butter and cheese. *Mozzarella alla caprese* is a simple but splendid salad of soft white buffalo cheese, tomatoes, olive oil, pepper and basil. For a profusion of tastes on one plate, sample *antipasto misto*, a miscellany of salami, olives, radishes, peppers, fennel, artichokes and pickled mushrooms.

Primo Piatto

Soups are not to be taken lightly; minestrone, a thick soup of mixed beans, vegetables, pasta and tomato sprinkled with parmesan cheese, is a far cry from the stuff you buy in a tin.

It might seem enough on its own, but a plate of pasta or risotto is usually only the first course, so loosen your belt and forget about the diet until after your trip.

The Piedmont is Italy's rice bowl, producing fine short-grain rice, and the variety of dishes that have resulted from this is truly impressive. Among the best, *risotto alla milanese* is cooked with onions, saffron and beef marrow; *risotto alla mantovana* with sausage and onion; *risotto alla certosina* has freshwater fish, shrimps, peas and mushrooms.

The other North Italian staple is *polenta*—cornmeal mush that can also be grilled or fried. In *polenta alla bergamasca*, it is served with sausage, tomato sauce and cheese. *Polenta e osei*, a Lombard speciality, is topped with roast game birds.

Local pasta dishes tend to be fairly heavy: *pizzoccheri*, buckwheat pasta with potatoes, cabbage, butter, cheese and sage; and *agnolini*, stuffed with meat, Parmesan and spices.

Secondo Piatto

The second course is typically a meat or fish dish, accompanied by potatoes or other vegetables. *Costoletta alla milanese* is a veal cutlet dipped in egg and breadcrumbs and fried in butter; the classic *osso buco* is thickly cut shin of veal gently braised in tomato sauce. Other regional dishes include *busecca*, a Milanese tripe stew, *cassoeula* (also spelt *cazzoeula*), stewed pork and cabbage, and *coniglio fritto alla lombarda*, rabbit fried in breadcrumbs.

The lakes provide a regular supply of freshwater fish. You'll find trout, carp, tench, perch and pike in restaurants around the region, with the favoured preparation serving them pan-fried and marinated in herbs.

Cheese and Dessert

There'll always be a plentifully stocked cheeseboard, with varieties from all over Italy. If you want to try some from the region,

go for the *parmigiano* (Parmesan), served in hard chunks; the blue-veined, pungent *gorgonzola*; or the smooth *taleggio*, creamy *mascarpone* or *Bel Paese*.

Italian desserts are a special treat. Sample the *torta di mele*, apple tart, or *zuppa inglese*, similar to English trifle. *Tiramisù* is a sponge, mascarpone, coffee and alcohol version that at its best is a delight.

Milan prides itself on being one of Italy's leading ice-cream centres, and the quality is reliably high. The classic Milanese *gelato* should be rich and creamy; connoisseurs favour the chocolate and hazelnut *gianduia*.

Wines

North Italy's flavoursome wines are a perfect match for the region's rich gastronomy. The vineyards around Lake Garda brim with fruity reds like Bardolino and Valpolicella, restrained rosés such as Chiaretto, and fine, dry whites, for instance Lugana. From Piedmont, to the west of Milan, comes the ruby-coloured Barolo, known as the "king of wines" by the locals, and great with meat and game, and the lively Barbera, best drunk young, and Grignolino.

Finish the meal Italian style with a bracing glass of *grappa* brandy, an *amaro*, or an aniseed-flavoured *sambuca*.

51

Recommended Restaurants

It's easy to find good traditional Italian food at almost any of the thousands of excellent local trattorias and restaurants in Milan and at the lake resorts. Those selected here offer the best in a range of Italian and Lombard cuisine, and at prices that won't break the bank.

Almost all of the Milanese restaurants are closed on Sunday, and many shut down for a couple of weeks in August. Those by the lakes tend to close, if at all, on Monday or Tuesday. They are generally open for lunch between 12 and 3 p.m., and again in the evening from 7.30 or 8 p.m. onwards. Phone to make check beforehand (dial the full number including the initial zero).

Al Buon Convento

Corso Italia 26, Milan
Tel. 02 864 535 46

In an old monastery of the historic centre, cosy, intimate atmosphere and Italian specialities.

Alla Cucina delle Langhe

Corso Como 6, Milan
Tel. 02 655 42 09

Lively local restaurant that serves good meat dishes, gnocchi and Piedmont wines.

Al Porto

Piazza Cantore, Milan
Tel. 02 894 074 25

Favoured as a power-lunch venue by Milanese businessmen. Especially known for its seafood.

Antica Trattoria della Pesa

Viale Pasubio 10, Milan
Tel. 02 655 57 41

Atmospheric fin de siècle decor in this trattoria where you can enjoy classic Lombard specialities such as *risotto* and *osso buco.*

Boeucc Antico Ristorante

Piazza Belgioioso 2, Milan
Tel. 02 760 202 24

Enjoy the romantic ambience at one of Milan's oldest restaurants. Specialities include *osso buco* with *risotto alla milanese* and *penne al branzino e zucchine.*

Il Garibaldi

Viale Monte Grappa 7, Milan
Tel. 02 659 80 06

Unflinchingly trendy, but highly traditional in its presentation of regional pasta and meat dishes.

I Matteoni

Piazza Cinque Giornate 6, Milan
Tel. 02 551 14 58

Frequented by discerning locals; excellent Tuscan cuisine.

Il Navigante

Via Magolfa 14, Milan
Tel. 02 894 063 20

South of Naviglio Grande, seafood and live music in a nautical setting.

Tasty grilled fish, straight out of the lake and into the dish.

La Cantina de Manuela
Via Mussi 13, Milan
Tel. 02 345 330 62
Wine bar where you can sample excellent salami and cheese with your glass.

La Scaletta
Piazza Stazione Porta
Genova 3, Milan
Tel. 02 581 002 90
Superb Italian nouvelle cuisine. Book a table; this is undoubtedly one of the best restaurants in Italy.

Le Biciclette Ristorante & Art Bar
Via Torti (corner Corso
Genova), Milan
Daily 6 p.m.–2 a.m., Saturday, Sunday brunch 12.30–4 p.m.
Tel. 02 581 043 25
Bar, restaurant, art and design exhibition all in one.

Nabucco
Via Fiori Chiari 10, Milan
Tel. 02 86 06 63
A smart but unpretentious restaurant in the Brera district that brings a touch of creativity to its salads, risottos, fish dishes and home-made desserts.

Oroscopo 91
Via P. da Volpedo 16, Milan
Tel. 02 498 33 21
Closed Monday

53

Two specialities here: fish, and the biggest pizzas in Milan, with toppings according to your zodiac sign.

Ristorante-Pizzeria Grand'Italia
Via Palermo 5, Milan
Tel. 02 87 77 59
This place in the Brera district serves huge slices of pizza.

Salernitano
Via Vitruvio 8, Milan
Tel. 02 295 256 82
Near the central railway station. Seafood specialities, such as the delicious *spaghetti al cartoccio*.

Santa Lucia
Via San Pietro all'Orto 3, Milan
Tel. 02 760 231 55
The fried baby squid is a treat; excellent pizza and pasta.

Savini
Galleria Vittorio Emanuele 2, Milan
Tel. 02 720 034 33
Milanese cuisine at its traditional best—but be prepared to pay for quality. Sample classic *risotto, osso buco* or *cassoeula*.

Trattoria all'Antica
Via Montevideo 4, Milan
Tel. 02 837 28 49
A good place to sample the delights of Lombardian cuisine.

Trattoria Bagutta
Via Bagutta 14, Milan
Tel. 02 760 009 02
Founded in 1927, this famous artists' haunt in the Monte Napoleone area has eye-catching murals. Excellent pasta and irresistible desserts.

Trattoria Madonnina
Via Gentilino 6, Milan
Tel. 02 894 090 89
A venerable restaurant serving traditional cuisine. Everything is home-made.

Trattoria Milanese
Via Santa Marta 11, Milan
Tel. 02 864 519 91
A cosy, family-run restaurant that's noted for its range of Lombardy's famous risottos.

Bilacus
Via Serbelloni 32
Bellagio, Lake Como
Tel. 031 95 04 80
Centrally located and serving fresh lake fish.

La Busciona
Via Vallassina 161
Bellagio, Lake Como
Tel. 031 96 48 31
Great local cuisine and a fabulous view of the lake to match.

Rino
Via Vitani 3, Como
Tel. 031 27 30 28

Classic Italian cuisine in the centre of Como.

Ristorante Teatro Sociale

Via Maestri Comacini 8
Como
Tel. 031 26 40 42

Good quality tourist restaurant handily situated in the vicinity of the cathedral.

Sant'Anna 1907

Via Turati 3
Como
Tel. 031 50 52 66

Pricey but first-rate Lombard cooking, particularly good for risotto, veal and trout.

Al Porticciolo 84

Via Fausto Valsecchi 5
Lecco, Lake Como
Tel. 0341 49 81 03

The best restaurant in town specializes in seafood and pasta. Delightful setting, even better in summer when the garden is open.

Vecchia Varenna

Contrada Scoscesa 10
Varenna, Lake Como
Tel. 0341 83 07 93

Mouth-watering haute cuisine with a seafood flavour, with the bonus of fantastic views.

Esplanade

Via Lario 10
Desenzano del Garda
Tel. 030 914 33 61

A beautiful lakeside garden adds to the gustatory pleasures of a fine seafood menu and impressive wine cellar.

Trattoria Cavallino

Via Murachette 21
Desenzano del Garda
Tel. 030 912 02 17

Well-known for its creative use of lake fish and game birds such as pigeon, quail and duck.

La Tortuga

Via XXIV Maggio 5
Gargnano, Lake Garda
Tel. 0365 712 51

In a fine setting by the port, this restaurant boasts a sophisticated combination of meat and fish dishes, plus exquisite desserts and wines.

Antica Trattoria alle Rose

Via Gasparo da Salò 93
Salò, Lake Garda
Tel. 0365 432 20

Cosy and hospitable atmosphere in which to enjoy many lake-fish specialities.

Trattoria Lacampagnoladisaló

Via Brunati 11
Salò, Lake Garda
Tel. 0365 221 53

Superb things are done here with home-made pasta, fresh vegetables and wild mushrooms. The house *tiramisù* is a scrumptious work of art.

55

Signori
Via Romagnoli 23
Sirmione, Lake Garda
Tel. 030 91 60 17
Scenic location by the lake and a good selection of tasty lake-fish dishes.

Vecchia Lugana
Piazzale Vecchia Lugana 1
Sirmione, Lake Garda
Tel. 030 91 90 12
Only ingredients in season are used in delicious fare that is prepared and presented with imagination and style.

Serenella
Feriolo
Lake Maggiore
Tel. 0323 281 12
Traditional fish and meat dishes and tasty home-made pasta.

Antica Stallera
Via Paolo Zaccheo 7
Cannobio, Lake Maggiore
Tel. 0323 715 95
Small hotel restaurant with a convivial atmosphere, with a hearty regional cuisine and an extensive selection of local wines.

Il Torchio
Via Manzoni 20
Pallanza, Lake Maggiore
Tel. 0323 50 33 52
Relaxed and homely setting for excellent cuisine that includes rabbit, duck, pigeon and lake fish.

Milano
Corso Zanitello 2
Pallanza, Lake Maggiore
Tel. 0323 55 68 16
There's no escaping lake fish in this region. Here they are prepared imaginatively, and the lakeside location is both elegant and delightful.

Rosa dei Venti
Corso Italia 50
Stresa, Lake Maggiore
Tel. 0323 314 31
Succulent pizzas and fabulous home-made pasta dishes with tomato or vegetable sauce.

Ristorante del Pescatore
Vicolo del Poncivo 3
Stresa, Lake Maggiore
Tel. 0323 319 86
Small family-run restaurant specializing in lake-fish dishes. Delicious lemon tart.

Chez Manuel
Via di Mezzo
Isola dei Pescatori
Borromean Islands
Tel. 0323 301 41
Small restaurant with garden. One of the specialities is spaghetti with a sauce of lake fish.

Verbano
Isola dei Pescatori
Borromean Islands
Tel. 0323 304 08
Fine traditional cuisine.

The Hard Facts

Airports

The region is served by two main airports. Malpensa, the larger of the two, lies 50 km (30 miles) northwest of Milan and receives mainly intercontinental flights, while Linate, only 8 km (5 miles) to the east, concentrates on domestic and European travel. Both airports provide banking, car-hire and information facilities, along with restaurants and duty-free shops.

From Linate, there's a frequent STAM shuttle bus service to Milan's Stazione Centrale. You can also take the ATM (Azienda Trasporti Milanesi) city bus no. 73 to Piazza San Babila in the centre of town, where there's a Metro station. Air Pullman coaches run regularly between Malpensa and Stazione Centrale with a journey time of approximately 1 hour. For flight information at both airports, telephone (02) 748 522 00.

Climate

Summer in Milan can be stiflingly hot, while the lakes usually offer a fresher climate. In winter, however, the city will often seem as icily cold as any in the north of Europe and it's always worth bringing along some warm clothing. Fortunately, the proximity of the Alps creates a benevolent micro-climate in certain parts of the lakes; the mountains act as a barrier to snow and rain clouds and you may find that you will be able to bask in warm sunshine outside a café in the middle of December. Probably the best time to be in the region is either spring or autumn, when there are fewer tourists to compete with, and the climate is consistently mild. In both these seasons, though, be prepared for some rain.

Communications

Stamps can be bought at post offices and at tobacconists (tabacchi). The main post office in Milan is at Piazza Cordusio and is open 24 hours a day.

International calls can be made from public phones, which all use phone cards (scheda telefonica). You have to tear off the corner before you first use them. Always happy with the latest fashions, the Milanese have taken to mobile phones, faxes and e-mail with gusto, and there should be little problem finding these services available if you need them.

The country code for Italy if you are calling from abroad is 39.

All Milan phone numbers begin with 02, which you have to dial whether you are in Milan or not. Towns around the lakes have their own prefixes, and it's best to contact Italian directory enquiries (tel. 12) for further information.

To call overseas from Italy, dial 00, the country code (1 for US and Canada, 44 for UK), then the area code (minus the initial 0) and the local number.

Consulates

Australia, Canada, Great Britain and the US all maintain consulates in Milan (the main embassies are in Rome). These should only be contacted in case of serious emergencies, lost passports or worse, and not for lost tickets or money.

Customs

EU regulations apply. For EU nationals over the age of 17, there is no limit on the import of duty-paid goods for personal consumption. There is an official import allowance duty-free of 200 cigarettes or 100 cigars or 250 g of tobacco and 1 litre of spirits plus 2 bottles of wine.

Driving

Milan's volume of traffic, the one-way systems and range of restrictions placed upon cars in the centre can be the stuff of nightmares. For sightseeing purposes, the city is best negotiated on foot or by public transport. It's wise to save hiring a car until you're heading out to the lakes.

Driving outside Milan is relatively straightforward. The motorways *(autostrada)* in Northern Italy are well-signposted, fast and direct ways to get around, though they are toll roads and the charges soon add up if you use them a lot. The roads that wind around the lakes are slow, narrow and extremely scenic. Unless you're on a tour coach, a car is a necessity for enjoying the lakes to the full.

The speed limit on motorways is 130 kph, 110 kph on large highways, 50 kph in built-up areas and 90 kph on other roads.

Petrol stations on the *autostrada* are usually open 24 hours; elsewhere, you'll find they probably close for lunch (noon to 3 p.m.), finish business for the day at 7 or 7.30 p.m., and only accept cash. At the pump, leaded petrol is *benzina*, unleaded is *benzina verde* or *senza piombo* and diesel is *gasolio*.

Car rental isn't cheap in Italy, and if you haven't already pre-booked, it's always worth ringing around both the international and local car hire firms as there are often special deals on offer. Be sure to have with you a valid driving licence, passport and a credit card, which will save you having to pay a cash deposit. You generally need to be over 21 to rent a car, although it can be 25 in some cases. The major rental companies have offices at both Malpensa and Linate airports and at the Stazione Centrale. There should be little difficulty in picking up your car in central Milan and leaving it at the airport when you leave (you might even avoid the 12 per cent surcharge for cars hired at the airport).

For road travel information in Milan, call the Automobile Club of Italy (ACI) on 02 376771. For nationwide information, telephone 1518. The ACI roadside assistance number is 803 803. If you take your own car, check before you leave whether your own automobile club has a reciprocal agreement with the ACI, otherwise consider additional breakdown insurance to cover international travel. Car hire firms have their own arrangements for breakdowns—be clear on what they are before you set out.

Emergencies
24 hour emergency numbers:
Ambulance/first-aid 113
Carabinieri (police) 112
Fire Brigade 115

Formalities
Visitors will only require a valid passport, or national ID card in the case of EU citizens, to enter Italy. No visas are needed for North American, Australian and New Zealand citizens for stays of three months or less.

Health
Health care in Italy is generally of a high standard, and doctors, dentists and hospital staff are often able to speak some English. Travellers from EU countries and Australia can claim reciprocal health care from the Italian National Health Service, but should obtain the relevant form from their health authorities prior to departure. No such agreements exist with the US, Canada and New Zealand, so it's best to check whether your existing health insurance covers foreign travel. If not, consider taking out separate travel insurance.

If you are going to require specialized prescription medicines, take your own in case you cannot find the exact equivalent on the spot. Chemists *(farmacia)* mainly keep to normal shopping hours. There's a 24-hour service in the Stazione Centrale.

Holidays and Festivals
Be prepared to find banks, shops and galleries closed on the following public holidays:

January 1	New Year
January 6	Epiphany
March/April (movable)	Easter Monday
April 25	Liberation Day

May 1	Labour Day
August 15	Assumption Day
November 1	All Saints' Day
December 7 (Milan)	Feast Day of St Ambrose (Sant'Ambrogio), Milan's Patron Saint
December 8	Immaculate Conception
December 25	Christmas Day
December 26	St Stephen's Day

There are religious, sporting and cultural festivals during almost every month of the year in Milan and the surrounding region. Check at the tourist office for what's on when you arrive.

Languages

Staff at most large hotels, shops and restaurants in Milan and around the lakes will speak some English, French or German. But don't be worried about having a bash at a few basic words or greetings in Italian as it always goes down well.

Media

The local Milan daily newspaper (though distributed nationwide) is the authoritative *Corriere della Sera*. The other main Italian paper is the more leftward-leaning *La Repubblica*, published in Rome. Both have a useful listings section for what's on in Milan. However, the paper most visible on the Milan metro is the pink daily *La Gazzetta dello Sport*.

British and other European newspapers and overseas editions of the International Herald Tribune and Wall Street Journal are readily available in Milan and at the main tourist resorts around the lakes.

Television broadcasts are entirely in Italian (foreign films and shows will invariably be dubbed). Larger hotels may have satellite TV with BBC, CNN, and various European channels. BBC World Service and Voice of America can be listened to with a short-wave radio.

Money

The Italian unit of currency is the Euro, divided into 100 cents (*centesimi*). Coins: 1, 2, 5, 10, 20 and 50 cents, 1 and 2 euros; banknotes: 5, 10, 20, 50, 100, 200 and 500 euros.

You can draw cash with your ordinary cash card, or with your Visa or Master Card at most cashpoint machines, as long as you know the PIN (personal identification number).

Credit cards are accepted at all major hotels, and most restaurants and shops—look for the *CartaSi* sign to be sure. For the best value on exchange rate and commission, cash your travellers cheques at a bank, not forgetting your passport for identification.

Opening hours

The following times are a general guide and subject to local variations. Bear in mind that virtually the whole of Milan pulls down the shutters for the steamy month of August and heads for the lakes or the coast.

Banks open Monday to Friday 8.30 a.m.–1 or 1.30 p.m., and 2.30 or 3–4 p.m.

Most shops open Monday to Saturday 9 a.m.–1 p.m. and 3.30 –7.30 p.m., though you may find food shops closed on Monday mornings and some other shops on Monday afternoons; in some places they close one day during the week.

Hours for museums, galleries and historic sites vary, but generally they open at 9 or 9.30 a.m. and all but the biggest will close for lunch. (Some don't reopen till the next day, so it's best to go in the morning if possible.) Museums often close on Mondays. Check with the local tourist information office before setting off anywhere too remote, as opening hours in Italy have a habit of changing.

Public Transport

Metro, buses and trams. The metro is probably the easiest way to navigate around Milan, and will whisk you quickly to all the main tourist spots. Entrances to stations are marked by a large red M. Open daily from 6 a.m. to midnight. Milan's ATM also runs a large network of buses and superb old trams that trundle around the city –pick up a map from the tourist office as the routes are difficult to understand.

Tickets are valid for the metro, buses and trams, and you can travel on the network for 75 minutes after they've been stamped. Single tickets or carnets of 10 can be bought at metro stations, tobacconists and newspaper kiosks. One-, two- or three-day passes are very economical if you are planning to travel around town a lot.

Trains. The Italian railway company is FS (Ferrovie dello Stato), and provides a frequent and inexpensive service from Milan to other major Italian cities, as well as nearby towns such as Pavia, Bergamo, Varese, Stresa and Como. The trains are often very busy, so either reserve a seat or turn up in plenty of time. For train information, tel. 89 20 21.

Taxis. Milan's white or yellow cabs wait outside major railway stations, large hotels, main piazzas and in the Piazza del Duomo. Fares around town are reasonable, but make sure the meter is running, and avoid hiring one to take you to the airport.

Boats. The main lakes have an enjoyable range of car-ferry, hydrofoil and paddle-steamer services. For further information on Lake Como call the Navigazione Lago di Como in Como on 031 30 40 60; for Lake Maggiore contact the Navigazione Lago Maggiore in Arona on 0322 242 352; or for Lake Garda telephone the Navigazione sul Lago di Garda in Desenzano on 030 914 95 11.

Safety

Serious crime aimed at tourists is rare in Italy. However, pickpockets and purse-snatchers operate in crowded areas such as metros and big sightseeing spots. The best plan is to take a few sensible precautions that will reduce the likelihood of being targeted in the first place. Keep wallets, cameras and handbags securely fastened and as much out of sight as possible. Place valuables, passports, etc. in the hotel safe. Don't carry large sums of money (bring travellers cheques or a bank card with which you can obtain local currency from cashpoints. Separate what you do have into smaller amounts and put them in different pockets. When travelling by train keep a close eye on your luggage.

Tipping

A service charge and VAT will be added to almost all restaurant bills, but it is usual to leave an extra tip of between 5 and 10 per cent as well. It is also customary to tip doormen, porters (about 1

euro per bag), hotel maids (1 euro per day) and taxi drivers (around 10 per cent).

Toilets

Public conveniences, called *toilette* or *gabinetto*, are generally in a decent condition in this part of Italy. If you make use of the facilities in a bar or restaurant, bear in mind that it is customary to order at least a drink before doing so. Men's toilets are signposted *Signori*, women's *Signore*, or with the usual silhouettes.

Tourist Information Offices

The main tourist offices in Milan are at Via Marconi 1, on the south side of the Duomo, and on the upper floor of the Stazione Centrale. They provide invaluable information on museum opening ours. You will also find offices at all the major tourist towns around the lakes. In Como there are two, at Piazza Cavour 17 and at Piazza A. Volta 54. Menaggio's is at Piazza Garibaldi and Stresa's at the landing stage, opposite the Town Hall.

Voltage

Most electric outlets are 220-volt 50 cycle A.C., although a few are 125 volts, and sockets are for plugs with two round pins. Take a travel plug and adapters for any sensitive equipment such as personal computers.

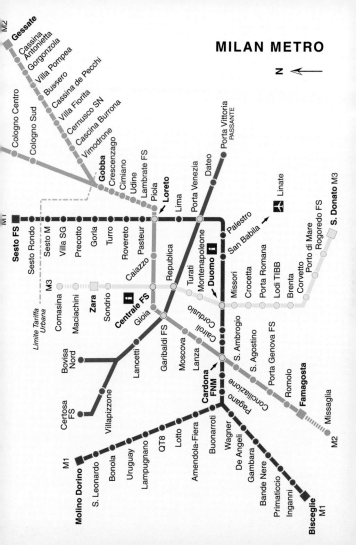

MILAN METRO

N ←

INDEX

GENERAL EDITOR
  Barbara Ender-Jones
LAYOUT
  Luc Malherbe
PHOTO CREDITS
  Cole Group, p. 2;
  Polis/Bersani, pp. 12, 18,
  22, 27 (bottom), 53;
  Polis/Perotti, p. 27 (top);
  Hémisphères/Lescourret,
  pp. 6, 10, 49;
  Hémisphères/Giulio, p. 32;
  Reinhard Balzerek, p. 41
MAPS
  Elsner & Schichor;
  Huber Kartographie;
  JPM Publications

Copyright © 2004, 1999
by JPM Publications S.A.
12, avenue William-Fraisse,
1006 Lausanne, Switzerland
E-mail:
information@jpmguides.com
Web site:
http://www.jpmguides.com/

All rights reserved. No part of this book may be reproduced or transmitted in any form or by any means, electronic or mechanical, including photocopying, recording or by any information storage and retrieval system without permission in writing from the publisher.

Every care has been taken to verify the information in the guide, but neither the publisher nor his client can accept responsibility for any errors that may have occurred. If you spot an inaccuracy or a serious omission, please let us know.

Printed in Switzerland
Weber/Bienne (CTP) — 04/02/01
Edition 2004–2005

Say it in Italian

Greetings

The Italians appreciate your greeting them with a *"buon giorno"* (literally "good day") or *"buona sera"* ("good evening"). Save *"buona notte"* ("good night") for when you're off to bed. Add *"come sta?"* ("how are you?") and your Italian had better be good enough to understand the answer. With luck, your accent will give you away and  people will be kind enough just to answer *"bene, grazie"* ("well, thank you") and not give you a rundown on their ailments and tax problems. If they are the first to ask, reply: *"Bene, grazie"* and add: *"E lei?"* ("And you?"). The proper response to *"grazie"* by itself is *"prego"* ("don't mention it"). Make your way through a crowded bus with a polite *"Permesso"* ("May I?").

Men and women shake hands on a first meeting. With a woman, once you've struck up a friendship, exchange a light kiss on each cheek, usually an airy affair to avoid lipstick marks or misunderstandings. Down south, men commonly exchange a Godfatherly bearhug. It's quite harmless.

DON'T BE SHY

To help you with your spoken Italian we provide a very simple transcription alongside the phrases. You may not end up sounding like a native speaker but people will be pleased to hear you trying. Syllables in capital letters should be stressed.

Good morning/ afternoon.	Buon giorno.	bwohn JOHR-noh
Good evening.	Buona sera.	BWOH-nah SEH-rah
Goodbye.	Arrivederci.	ahr-ree-veh-DEHR-chee
See you later.	A più tardi.	ah pyoo TAHR-dee
Hi!/Bye!	Ciao!	CHAA-oh
Yes/No.	Sì/No.	see/noh
Maybe.	Forse.	FOHR-seh
That's fine/Okay.	D'accordo.	dah-KOHR-doh
That's right!	Va bene.	vah BEH-neh
Please.	Per favore.	pehr fah-VAW-reh
Thank you/Thanks.	Grazie.	GRAA-tsyeh
Thank you very much.	Tante grazie.	TAHN-teh GRAA-tsyeh
You're welcome.	Prego.	PREH-goh
Nice to meet you.	Molto lieto.	MOHL-toh LYEH-toh
How are you?	Come sta?	KAW-meh stah
Well, thanks.	Bene, grazie.	BEH-neh, GRAA-tsyeh
And you?	E lei?	eh lay
Pardon me.	Mi scusi.	mee SKOO-zee
I'm sorry.	Mi dispiace.	mee dee-SPYAA-cheh
Don't mention it.	Non c'è di che.	nohn cheh dee keh
Excuse me…	Scusi…	SKOO-zee
My name is…	Mi chiamo…	mee KYAA-moh
I don't understand.	Non capisco.	nohn kah-PEE-skoh
Slowly, please.	Parli piano.	PAHR-lee PYAA-noh
Could you say that again?	Può ripetere, per favore?	pwoh ree-PEH-teh-reh, pehr fah-VAW-reh
Do you speak English?	Parla inglese?	PAHR-lah eeng-GLEH-zeh
I don't speak much Italian.	Non parlo bene l'italiano.	nohn PAHR-loh BEH-neh lee-tah-LYAA-noh
Please write it down.	Per favore, me lo scriva.	pehr fah-VAW-reh, meh loh SKREE-vah
I understand.	Capisco.	kah-PEE-skoh
Let's go.	Andiamo.	ahn-DYAA-moh

Getting around

Official metered yellow taxis line up at railway stations or outside the major hotels, only rarely hailed when they are on the move. Beware of pirate drivers, identifiable by the fact that *they* approach you. Unauthorized cars are called in Italian *abusivi*, which says it all. Expect legitimate extras on the meter price, charged particularly on night trips, on several pieces of luggage or on rides to or from the airport—rates are posted in the vehicle. Add a 10 per cent tip.

Public transport. Services for the bus *(autobus)* vary—they are good in Florence and Milan, overcrowded in Rome and Naples. The water-bus in Venice *(vaporetto* or smaller, faster *motoscafo)* is best of all—like a cheerful cruise along the canals through centuries of history. The number of the bus lines and the route served are displayed at each bus stop *(fermata)*. For cheaper fares, buy a book of tickets *(blocchetto di biglietti)* at news-stands or tobacconists. Get on through the door marked *"Salita"* and off at the exit marked *"Uscita"*. Subway trains, *Metro(politano)*, operate in Milan and Rome; the tickets are interchangeable with the bus system.

Trains. Besides the luxury international *EuroCity* (EC) and the *Intercity* (IC), there's the *Rapido*, faster than the crowded *Espresso*. The *Diretto* is slower and the *Locale* slower still, stopping at every halt, seemingly for anyone who cares to whistle it down.

Taxi, please!	Taxi!	TAH-ksee
Are you free?	È libero?	eh LEE-beh-roh
Hotel Paradiso, please.	Hotel Paradiso, per favore.	oh-TEHL pah-rah-DEE-zoh, pehr fah-VAW-reh
To the airport/ the station, please.	All'aeroporto/ alla stazione, per favore.	ahl-lah-eh-roh-POHR-toh/ AHL-lah stah-TSYAW-neh, pehr fah-VAW-reh
I'm in a hurry.	Ho fretta.	oh FREHT-tah
Please stop here.	Si fermi qui.	see FEHR-mee kwee
Please wait for me.	Aspetti un momento, per favore.	ah-SPEHT-tee oon moh-MEHN-toh, pehr fah-VAW-reh
How much is it?	Quant'è?	kwahn-TEH
Keep the change.	Tenga il resto.	TEHNG-gah eel REH-stoh
Where is the bus stop?	Dov'è la fermata dell'autobus?	daw-VEH la fer-MAH-tah dehl-LA-oo-toh-boos
When does the next bus leave?	Quando parte il prossimo bus?	KWAHN-doh PAR-teh eel PROHS-see-moh boos
Where is the metro, please?	Dov'è il metrò, per favore?	daw-VEH eel meh-TROH, pehr fah-VAW-reh
A book of tickets, please.	Un blocchetto di biglietti, per favore.	oon blohk-KEHT-toh dee bee-LYEHT-tee, pehr fah-VAW-reh
one-way	andata	ahn-DAA-tah
round-trip	andata e ritorno	ahn-DAA-tah eh ree-TOHR-noh
first class	prima classe	PREE-mah KLAHS-seh
second class	seconda classe	seh-KOHN-dah KLAHS-seh
platform	binario	bee-NAA-ryoh
toilets	gabinetti	gah-bee-NEHT-tee
Is this seat free?	È libero questo posto?	eh LEE-beh-roh KWEH-stoh POH-stoh
strike	sciopero	SHOH-peh-roh

Accommodation

Your hotel lobby is where you first learn how much Italians like their titles. You'll get better service if you call the hall-porter or bell-captain *portiere,* as opposed to *facchino* (baggage porter or bellhop). Upstairs, the room maid is *cameriera.* Hotel tipping also has its fine distinctions: on the spot to porters for carrying bags or other incidental services, but a lump sum to room maids at the end of the stay.

Ratings for the hotel *(hotel* or *albergo)* range from luxury five-star to rudimentary one-star. Expect in-house laundry and dry-cleaning services only from three-star and better. Breakfast is generally optional (and not particularly copious) but in high season, resort hotels often insist on at least half-board. A separate rating system is used for boarding houses *(pensione),* ranging from very comfortable, with excellent family cooking, to modest, providing just the basic services. Humble accommodation in monasteries run by monks is very different from the often luxurious amenities of converted monasteries run by hoteliers.

If you have checked out of your hotel, you can still take a *siesta* and bath in a low-price day hotel *(albergo diurno),* usually close to the main railway station.

I've a reservation	Ho fatto una prenotazione	oh FAHT-toh oo-nah preh-noh-ta-TSYAW-neh
Here's the confirmation/voucher.	Ecco la conferma/il buono.	EHK-koh lah kohn-FEHR-mah/ eel BWAW-noh
a single room	una camera singola	OO-nah KAA-meh-rah SEENG-goh-lah
a double	una camera doppia	OO-nah KAA-meh-rah DOHP-pyah
twin beds	letti gemelli	LEHT-tee jeh-MEHL-lee
double bed	letto matrimoniale	LEHT-toh mah-tree-moh-NYAA-leh
with a bath/shower	con bagno/doccia	kohn BAH-nyoh/ DOHT-chah
Can I see the room?	Posso vedere la camera?	POHS-so veh-DEH-reh lah KAH-meh-rah
My key, please.	La mia chiave, per favore.	lah MEE-ah KYAA-veh, pehr fah-VAW-reh
Is there mail for me?	C'è posta per me?	cheh POH-stah pehr meh
I need: hangers soap a blanket an (extra) pillow	Ho bisogno di: grucce una saponetta una coperta un guanciale (in più)	oh bee-ZAW-nyoh dee GROOT-che OO-nah sah-poh-NEHT-tah OO-nah koh-PEHR-tah oon gwahn-CHAA-leh (een pyoo)
This is for the laundry.	Questo è da lavare.	KWEH-stoh eh dah lah-VAA-reh
These are clothes to be cleaned/ pressed. Urgently.	Questi sono vestiti da pulire/ stirare. È urgente.	KWEH-stee SAW-noh veh-STEE-tee dah poo-LEE-reh/stee-RAA-reh eh oor-JEHN-teh
I'm checking out. I'd like to pay by credit card	Lascio l'albergo. Vorrei pagare con carta di credito.	LAHSH-shoh lahl-BEHR-goh vohr-RAY pah-GAA-reh kohn KAHR-tah dee KREH-dee-toh

Buon appetito!

The advantage of the ordinary *trattoria* restaurant over the more formal (and higher priced) establishment known as a *ristorante* is usually apparent as soon as you walk in. Much of the day's "menu" is appetizingly laid out on a long table or refrigerated counter. The display includes not only cold starters *(antipasti)* but also fish *(pesce)* or other seafood *(frutti di mare)* and even cuts of meat *(carne)*. State your cooking preference: *alla griglia* (grilled), *fritto* (fried) or *al forno* (baked). The *pasta* of course is in the kitchen, but these days it comes in literally hundreds of different shapes and sizes—manufacturers even have architects to design new forms to enhance the different sauces.

At midday, you may prefer the stand-up bar known as *tavola calda,* where you can get sandwiches and a hot or cold dish at the counter. Better than fast-food is the *panino ripieno,* a bread roll stuffed with cold meats, sausage, salad or cheese—your personal choice from the counter-display—the original of the American "submarine".

YOU AND YOU

There are several ways of saying "you" in Italian. *Tu* (plural *voi*) is familiar, used for children, friends, family. *Lei* (plural *loro*) is polite, for people you don't know well. And if you meet the person of your dreams, "I love you" is *Ti amo.*

I'm hungry/thirsty.	**Ho fame/sete.**	oh FAA-meh/SEH-teh
A table for two, please.	**Un tavolo per due, per favore.**	oon TAA-voh-loh pehr DOO-eh, pehr fa-VAW-reh
The menu	**Il menù**	eel meh-NOO
The fixed menu	**Il menú fisso**	eel mch-NOO FFES-soh
I'm a vegetarian.	**Sono vegetariano(a).**	SAW-noh veh-jeh-tah-RYAA-noh(ah)
A glass of water.	**Un bicchiere d'acqua.**	oon-beek-KYEH-reh DAHK-kwah
I'd like a beer.	**Vorrei una birra.**	vohr-RAY oo-nah BEER-rah.
The wine list.	**La carte dei vini.**	lah KAHR-tah day VEE-nee
A bottle of red/white/rosé wine.	**Una bottiglia di vino rosso/bianco/rosato.**	oo-nah boht-TEE-lyah dee VEE-noh ROHS-soh/BYANG-koh/roh-ZAA-toh
beef	**manzo**	MAHN-dzoh
bread	**pane**	PAA-neh
butter	**burro**	BOOR-roh
cheese	**formaggio**	fohr-MAHD-joh
chicken	**pollo**	POHL-loh
coffee	**caffè**	kahf-FEH
fish	**pesce**	PEHSH-sheh
fruit juice	**succo di frutta**	SOOK-koh dee FROOT-tah
ice cream	**gelato**	jeh-LAA-toh
meat	**carne**	KAHR-neh
milk	**latte**	LAHT-teh
mineral water	**acqua minerale**	AHK-kwah mee-neh-RAA-leh
fizzy/flat	**gasata/naturale**	gah-ZAA-tah/nah-too-RAA-leh
mustard	**senape**	SEH-nah-peh
pork	**maiale**	mah-YAA-leh
salt and pepper	**sale e pepe**	SAA-leh eh PEH-peh
tea	**tè**	teh
vegetables	**verdura**	vehr-DOO-rah
The bill	**Il conto**	eel KOHN-toh

Telephone

You'll soon notice that on the telephone, the Italians do not reply with *Buon giorno* but *"Pronto!"* It means literally that the caller is "ready" to speak, a national characteristic. If you are answering the phone, in all likelihood, your next phrase should be *"Parla inglese?"* ("Do you speak English?") If the answer is *"No"*, try *"Qui parla..."* ("This is ... speaking").

Italy now has a modern, privatized telephone network, and just about everybody walks around talking into a mobile phone. Public telephones *(cabina telefonica)* function with phone cards, which can be purchased at post offices, some newspaper kiosks, the headquarters of Italian telecommunications and railway stations. They do not work until you tear off the corner. There are also Internet Cafés in every town, so you can keep in touch with your e-mails.

To call the US and Canada direct, dial 001. For the UK, the country code is 0044. Note that for local calls, you have to dial the whole number, including the initial 0.

May I use this phone?	Posso usare questo telefono?	POHS-soh oo-ZAA-reh KWEH-stoh teh-LEH-foh-noh
Can I reverse the charges?	Posso telefonare a carico del destinatario?	POHS-soh teh-leh-foh-NAA-reh ah KAA-ree-koh dehl deh-stee-nah-TOH-ryoh

---

HAPPY TALK

Enrich your vocabulary and sprinkle your conversation with a few useful, cheery adjectives: *simpatico* (charming), *splendido* (magnificent), *fantastico* (terrific), *formidabile* (tremendous), *divertente* (amusing), *piacevole* (pleasant), *allegro* (happy).

Wrong number.	Numero sbagliato.	NOO-meh-roh zbah-LYAA-toh
Speak more slowly.	Parli più piano.	PAHR-lee pyoo PYAA-noh
Could you take a message?	Può prendere un messaggio?	pwoh PREHN-deh-reh oon mehs-SAHD-joh
My number is…	Il mio numero è il…	eel MEE-oh NOO-meh-roh eh eel
My room number is…	Il mio numero di camera è il…	eel MEE-oh NOO-meh-roh dee KAA-meh-rah eh eel
Do you sell stamps?	Avete dei francobolli?	ah-VEH-teh day frahng-koh-BOHL-lee
How much is it to Great Britain/ the United States?	Quanto è per la Gran Bretagna/ gli Stati Uniti?	KWAHN-toh eh pehr lah grahn breh-TAH-nyah/ lyee STAA-tee oo-NEE-tee
I'd like to mail this parcel.	Vorrei spedire questo pacco.	vohr-RAY speh-DEE-reh KWEH-sto PAHK-koh
Can I send a fax?	Posso mandare un fax?	POHS-soh mahn-DAA-reh oon fahks
Can I make a photocopy here?	Posso fare una fotocopia qui?	POHS-soh FAA-reh OO-nah foh-toh-KAW-pyah kwee
Where's the mailbox?	Dov'è la cassetta delle lettere?	daw-VEH lah kahs-SEHT-tah DEHL-leh LEHT-teh-reh
registered letter	lettera raccomandata	LEHT-teh-rah rahk-kohm-mahn-DAA-tah
air mail	via aerea	VEE-ah ah-EH-reh-ah
postcard	cartolina postale	kahr-toh-LEE-nah poh-STAA-leh

NUMBERS			
1 uno	6 sei	11 undici	16 sedici
2 due	7 sette	12 dodici	17 diciassette
3 tre	8 otto	13 tredici	18 diciotto
4 quattro	9 nove	14 quattordici	19 diciannove
5 cinque	10 dieci	15 quindici	20 venti

Money matters

Italy has adopted the Euro, and it makes life simple (it's just like using dollars). Coins are issued in denominations of 1, 2, 5, 10, 20 and 50 euro cents *(centesimi)*, 1 and 2 euros. Banknotes: 5, 10, 20, 50, 100, 200 and 500 euros.

The better exchange rate you get at the bank compared with the hotel is offset by the amount of time spent waiting in line, often one to make the initial transaction and another to collect the cash. Have your passport with you. In most places, banks are open Monday to Friday, 8.30 a.m. to 1.30 p.m. and another hour in mid-afternoon. Railway station and airport currency exchange offices stay open longer, and weekends as well. Most convenient of all – as long as you know your PIN – are the automatic cash dispensers for international credit cards (at stations and main tourist centres), but you will have to pay a commission.

QUESTION MARK

To ask a question in Italian, all you have to do is change the inflexion of your voice, lifting it towards the end of the sentence:

It's far away.	**È lontano.**
It's far?	**È lontano**?

bank	banca	BAHN-kah
currency exchange	cambio	KAHM-byoh
Where can I change money?	Dove posso cambiare del denaro?	DAW-veh POHS-soh kahm-BYAA-reh dehl dch NAA-roh
Can you cash a travellers cheque?	Può incassare un travellers cheque?	pwoh een-kahs-SAA-reh oon "travellers check"
I want to change dollars/pounds.	Voglio cambiare dei dollari/ delle sterline.	VOH-lyoh kahm-BYAA-reh day DOHL-lah-ree/ DEHL-leh stehr-LEE-neh
Will this credit card do?	Accetta questa carta di credito?	aht-CHEHT-tah KWEH-stah KAHR-tah dee KREH-dee-toh
Can you help me?	Può aiutarmi?	pwoh ah-yoo-TAAR-mee
Just looking…	Sto solo guardando...	stoh SAW-loh gwahr-DAHN-doh
How much is this?	Quant'è?	kwahn-TEH
cheap	buon mercato	bwohn mehr-KAA-toh
expensive	caro	KAA-roh
Can I try it on?	Posso provarlo?	POHS-soh proh-VAHR-loh
I don't know the European sizes.	Non conosco le taglie europee.	nohn koh-NOH-skoh leh TAA-lyeh eh-oo-roh-PEH-eh
It's too big/small	È troppo grande/ piccolo.	eh trop-poh GRAN-deh/ PEE-koh-loh
I'll think about it.	Voglio pensarci.	VOH-lyoh pehn-SAHR-chee
I'll buy it.	Lo prendo.	loh PREHN-doh
A receipt, please.	Una ricevuta, per favore.	OO-nah ree-cheh-VOO-tah, pehr fah-VAW-reh
antique shop	antiquario	ahn-tee-KWAA-ryoh
bakery	panetteria	pah-neht-teh-REE-ah
bookshop	libreria	lib-reh-REE-ah
pharmacy	farmacia	fahr-mah-CHEE-ah
jewellery store	gioielleria	joh-yehl-leh-REE-ah
pastry shop	pasticceria	pah-steet-cheh-REE-ah
shoe shop	calzoleria	kal-tsoh-leh-REE-ah
supermarket	supermercato	soo-pehr-mehr-KAA-toh

Health and Safety

The best planned vacation may sometimes be spoiled-—by a stomach upset or something of the sort. Too much sun, too much Chianti in the middle of the day and you'll be looking around for the chemists *(farmacia)*. One of them is open somewhere in town, even nights and weekends. Most often, it's located near the main railway station.

If you're prone to something that needs special medication, take a supply from home since, as good as most Italian medicine is, you may not be able to find precisely the same prescription on the spot. The emergency number to dial for first aid is **118**, and for an ambulance **113**.

Safety First. There's no need to be paranoid, but it's silly to take pointless risks. The precautions are simple, and the same as in big towns anywhere in the world. Leave your valuables in the hotel's safe *(cassaforte)* and carry only as much cash as you need. Keep your passport separate from your travellers cheques and credit cards. If you have rented a car, don't park it with bags visible on the seats. Always be on the alert for pickpockets in crowded places.

Police come in two kinds: *Vigili Urbani* (municipal police) in navy blue uniforms or all white in summer; and *Carabinieri* in brown or black, handling major crimes and street-demonstrations.

Emergency number for the police: **112**

I don't feel well.	Non mi sento bene.	nohn mee SEHN-toh BEH-neh
Where is a chemists?	Dov'è una farmacia?	daw-VEH OO-nah fahr-mah-CHEE-ah
an upset stomach	un'indigestione	oon-een-dee-jeh-STYAW-neh
an injury	una ferita	OO-nah feh-REE-tah
toothache	mal di denti	mahl dee DEHN-tee
headache	mal di testa	mahl dee TEH-stah
I feel pain…	Mi fa male…	mee fah MAA-leh
… in my leg	… la gamba	lah GAHM-bah
… in my arm	… il braccio	eel BRAH-choh
… in my stomach	… lo stomaco	loh STOM-mah-koh
… in my chest	… il petto	eel PEHT-toh
I am bleeding.	Perdo sangue.	PEHR-doh SANG-gweh
I need a doctor.	Ho bisogno di un dottore.	oh bee-ZAW-nyoh dee oon doht-TAW-reh
Can you give me a prescription?	Può darmi una ricetta?	pwoh DAHR-mee OO-nah ree-CHEHT-tah
Help!	Aiuto!	ah-YOO-toh
Stop thief!	Al ladro!	ahl LAA-droh
Leave me alone.	Mi lasci in pace.	mee LASH-shee een PAA-cheh
I've lost my wallet/ passport.	Ho perso il portafogli/ il passaporto.	oh PEHR-soh eel pohr-tah FAW-lyee/ eel pahs-sah-POHR-toh
My credit cards have been stolen.	Mi hanno rubato le carte di credito.	mee AHN-noh roo-BAA-toh leh KAHR-teh dee KREH-dee-toh
I'm lost.	Mi sono perso.	mee SAW-noh PEHR-soh
Where's the police station/the hospital?	Dov'è la polizia/ l'ospedale?	daw-VEH lah poh-lee TSEE-ah/ loh-speh-DAA-leh
I have been assaulted.	Sono stato aggredito.	SAW-noh STAA-to ahg-greh-DEE-toh
witness	testimone	tes-tee-MOH-neh
lawyer	avvocato	av-voh-KAH-toh

Illustrations: Sofie Czaplejewicz

EVERY LETTER COUNTS

In Italian, every letter of the word is pronounced distinctly, so when a letter is doubled you have to pronounce it twice: *frutto* is "frut to", *delle* "del le", *birra* "bir ra", and so on.

NOTICES

The meaning of some signs you'll see:

Chiuso	Closed	*Signore (Donne)*	Ladies
Entrata (Ingresso)	Entrance	*Signori (Uomini)*	Gentlemen
Guasto	Out of order	*Uscita*	Exit
Occupato	Occupé	*Vietato*	Forbidden

FALSE FRIENDS

Many Italian words look like direct equivalents of English words, but you could be very wrong:

camera	room	*magazzino*	warehouse
conveniente	cheap, inexpensive	*moneta*	coins, change
fresco	cool	*morbido*	soft
incidente	accident	*pila*	battery (transistor)
libreria	bookstore	*slip*	underpants

JPM Publications • *Specialists in customized guides*

Neither the publisher nor his client can be held responsible in any way for omissions or errors.
Av. William-Fraisse 12, 1006 Lausanne, Suisse
Copyright© 2004, 1999 JPM Publications SA
www.jpmguides.com/ Printed in Switzerland – 0/402 – (CTP)